MAKING DELHI A BETTER PLACE
Promoting a Vision of Urban Renaissance

MAKING DELHI A BETTER PLACE

Promoting a Vision of Urban Renaissance

B.G. Fernandes

Publications

KALPAZ PUBLICATIONS

DELHI-110052

Making Delhi a Better Place
Promoting a Vision of Urban Renaissance

Rs. 690

ISBN : 81-7835-455-1

Published in 2006 in India by
Kalpaz Publications
C-30, Satyawati Nagar, Delhi-110052
E-mail : Kalpaz@hotmail.com

Laser Typesetting at : Master Computers, Delhi
Printed at : Salasar Imaging System, Delhi

FOR JOAN

Who Streadfastly Believed ....If you want

Something very badly, You got to make it happen.....

like making Delhi a Better Place to Live In

Contents

Preface

While Delhi is booming with economic prosperity, very little attention has been paid to environmental aspects of social and economic change, with the result Delhi has degenerated from being a gracious historic city to an urban blight.

When Delhi is faced with urban crisis of huge and growing proportions, that is affecting the well-being of its citizens, there is no political will, no urban strategy, no priority, and no direction in the systematic response to the crisis, from either the state government or the municipal bodies, or the Delhi Development Authority.

Neither the self-serving politicians nor the non-committed bureaucracy show any concern for urban improvement, while the urban environment is being destroyed for commercial greed and profit.

Inspite of four decades of urban planning, unchallenged application of the principles of Laissez-faire in the building and rebuilding of Delhi has created critical problems like traffic congestion, unsightliness, and intolerable living conditions.

The best reason for bringing out this book is to stimulate public concern for Delhi's deteriorating urban environment and of the profound effect it has on their daily life, and thus prepare ground for making Delhi a better place. Making Delhi a better place is a cause and like all causes its success depends on the contribution of many, rather than few.

It would take too much space to express my gratitude to all who have helped make this book possible. However, I thank my wife Joan for her quiet support for the book, she suspected I was working on. I am grateful to Manoj who ran the manuscript of the book through the word processor and did an excellent job. Also, I thank my publishers for the valuable inputs in the process of editing the book.

B.G. Fernandes

Introduction

When I boarded the Frontier Mail at Mumbai Central, that took me to New Delhi, nearly half-century ago, little did I realise that greater part of my life would be spent in the national Capital.

Coming from Mumbai, then the 'Urbs Prima in Indis, Delhi, gave an impression of no more than a 'glorified village', with the exception of New Delhi, the colonial city designed by Sir Edwin Lutyen, with its tree-lined avenues and spacious bungalows, resembling lifeless 'plantation living', in contrast to the vibrant walled-city of Delhi.

Like many new comers, I was at once attracted and repelled by Delhi, exhilarated by its history and diversity, but dismayed by the rawness and apparent disorder. For many, Delhi has always held special fascination, especially for those interested in cultural and architectural heritage.

My perception of Delhi was of a vast outdoor museum, replete with ancient monuments—the relics of bygone dynasties. For better or worse Delhi suited me pretty well. But, over the years Delhi has, progressively, made great strides towards utterly destroying its essential character in an absurd quest for growth.

Delhi, the capital of a great nation, has over the years become a cesspool of squalor, rot, confusion and shameless mismanagement, with reigning anarchy. And, all this is happening under the very nose—of central, state and local government.

Life in Delhi crawls by in an atmosphere of routine and frustration. Tension, hate, road-outrages and sadness have distorted the faces of persons riding overcrowded buses bursting at their seams. The overloaded civic services near collapse, power outages with rolling blackouts, have become endemic to the capital. Traffic gridlocks and polluted air have assumed hazardous proportions. Rising crimes have bred insecurity in the neighbourhoods.

Delhi, an already overburdened metropolis, keeps growing at an alarming rate, without direction, control or intelligently guided effort, threatening to become or has already become one big seamless, urban megalopolis.

Delhi represents the extreme example of what can happen when the country opens itself to the rush of global investment, without the necessary filters and surge protectors to regulate growth. The urban crisis of huge and growing proportions that has gripped the national capital, will have to be faced up to or ignored at our own peril. To quote President J.F. Kennedy: "We will neglect our cities to our peril, for in neglecting them we neglect the nation".

So much is happening so quickly and in such a big way, that alternative directions are urgent before we lose the opportunity to renew Delhi, and wind up only with more costly, less desirable options of replacement.

What is making the Capital of India less than the most desirable place to live? What is wrong with Delhi?

What kinds of problems exists, and why? How did Delhi reach this point? What has happened to this historic city? Answers to these questions will enable us to understand the evolution and the pathology of the national capital and to make the diagnosis of the situation.

It is clear, that neither the self-serving politicians nor the non-committed bureaucracy show any concern for urban improvement, while Delhi's urban environment is being progressively destroyed for the sake of profit and for satisfying commercial greed. It is also clear that the politician-bureaucrat-powercrat triumvirate will continue to gloss over Delhi's problem for short-term gains. We, the Delhiites, cannot wait until urban problems reach near-crisis proportions, before action is taken.

The Delhiites are paying for problems created in the past, over decades and may be generations. They cannot be solved overnight. It will take one or more generations to face them completely.

As responsible citizens of Delhi, we need to take charge of our city—the national capital. The representative governments both at State and City level will not work effectively, without some of the brave Delhiites, who are willing to put themselves and their resources on the line for good urban governance—a government that works for the welfare of the people. Those who are aware that Delhi is mired in serious difficulties, should be searching for ways to create a better place to live. We need a middle class and an elite with enough commitment to social activism. If you want something badly, you have to make it happen.

It is within our reach in this day and age, to create a healthy, pleasant, safe and people-friendly and stimulating urban environment in the national capital, using the tools of modern technology. Today, we live in an incredible age, an age where we have an opportunity to learn, to talk with each other, where we have a wonderful diversity that brings all types of perspectives to the table. The present is a time of great vitality. Our appetite for understanding has reached heights that our forefathers never imagined.

This is a time not for despair but for a commitment to make the most of our know how to address the problems we face in our daily lives. The problems may seem insurmountable, but they are not. I am sure, we have the tools, we have brilliant, dedicated people in the Capital to find answers. All we need is a sense of sharing and above all the will to change.

Making Delhi a better place to live and work in, should be of concern to all who have been relentlessly subjected to most deplorable and appalling living conditions in the nation's Capital. Making Delhi a better place is a cause, and like all causes its success depends on the contribution of many, rather than a few.

Some of us can point to cities that are uniquely special, that stand out in their distinctive character, charm, the way they function. Whether we think of these cities because of some nostalgic association or current everyday living, they seem to be ideal, in the way they have created and retained their significant character and resources, as they have changed and grown over time.

Delhi once had a special quality about it, but which since has become just another unrecognisable part of a larger amorphous sprawling metropolis. Perhaps, Delhiites are not demanding a better Delhi, because the choice has never been offered. They seem to accept what they have gotten used to live with, in a milieu of "Chalta hai" society. They cannot imagine anything else. It is necessary for the citizens of Delhi to understand the present catastrophy of their metropolis or they will never be able to see the vibrant opportunities for creating a better Delhi that lies before them.

For sometime now I have felt a strong desire to write a book about "Making Delhi a Better Place". What moves me to write, is the awareness of how important is that every inhabitant of Delhi should be seriously concerned about improving his or her quality of life.

The reason for this book is to reach out to every Delhiites, to galvanize them in getting actively involved in moving the local politicians and officials to act towards the goal of replanning, reshaping and rebuilding the national capital. For democracy to work requires peoples' involvement.

The complexity of present living conditions and the variety of factors that have caused the decay to Delhi's urban environment cannot be fully covered in a book of this type. Notwithstanding, the book brings into focus the pressing problems that need to be addressed urgently.

The problems Delhi is faced with are not simply the sum of separate problems. Rather, all of the issues are part of one system—a living, breathing metropolis. The system cannot be fixed by fixing one part at a time, instead we must take a holistic approach, that looks at the totality of what make up this vibrant metropolis of Delhi and address all these issue at once.

This book is not about a systematic study, but a more or less ordered gathering of impressions and ideas for reshaping our national capital and with it the lives of the people who live in it. It is an effort to understand the vast and varied man-made landscape that constitutes metropolitan Delhi and its environs.

The book offers some ideas and suggestions on how to make Delhi a better place, of what each of us can do to make our city more livable, sustainable and humane. A small step to rebuilding the kind of Delhi we would all like to be part of.

B.G. Fernandes

1

Delhi in Evolution

Delhi is a 450 years old capital of a string of empires, from the Pandavas Indraprastha to Sir Edwin Lutyen's New Delhi, with each new power creating its own city. The origin of the name of Delhi is lost in antiquity, and the city is known to have flourished under various names. Presumably, the corrupted names Dilli, Dehli, and finally Delhi were evolved after the name of Raja Dillu, a member of the Maurya Dynasty who reigned in the First Century B.C.

Ancient legend has it, that 'he who rules Delhi, rules India' and it is in recognition of this strategic position, that Delhi has been the ancient and historic Capital of India for Centuries. On the plains of Delhi are the ruins of six or more cities that at one time or another were the capitals of mighty kingdoms and empires. Delhi has an ancient history of splendour and squalor, of destruction and of persistent reconstruction. The environs of Delhi are the graveyards of the generations past. Here, numerous dynasties rose, ruled and perished.

Delhi's famous 'seven cities' range from the 12th Century Qila Rai Pithora, built by Prithviraj Chauhan, to the imperial walled-city built by Shahjahan, the Mughal emperor, in the 17th Century.

The first city of Delhi Qila Rai Pithora built by the Chauhans in about 1180, was captured by Qutub-ud-din Aibak in 1192, who established his capital there. The runins of this first city, lies near Mehrauli, which marked the last stronghold of Hindu rule in Delhi, for it was at that time in the 12th Century, after the defeat of Rai Pithora, that Delhi passed into Mughal hands, and remained until advent of the British Raj.

The second city, Siri was built by Alauddin Khilji in 1303, which can still be seen near the Siri Fort Auditorium and the near by village of Shahpur Jat.

The third city, Tughlaqabad a fort on the foothills of the Aravallis range, was built during Ghiyasuddin Tughlaqi's four-year reign from 1321–1325.

Jahanpanah, the fourth city, was built by Muhammad bin Thughlaqi from 1325 to 1351 as a walled enclosure to link Qila Rai Pithora and Siri. The ruins of this fourth city lie near Chirag-Delhi.

The fifth city Ferozabad, stretching north from Hauz Khas to the banks of the Yamuna River, was built by Feroze Shah Tughlaq—from 1351-1388.

Purana Qila, Delhi's Sixth city, Dinpanah, was built by Humayun, stands on an ancient site that has been continuously occupied since 1000 B.C. In 1540 the Purana Qila was captured by the Afghan Chieftan Sher Shah Suri, who named it Shergarh.

Shahjahanabad–the walled city of Delhi, was the seventh city, built between 1638 and 1649 by Emperor

Shahjahan, who shifted the Mughal capital here from Agra.

Delhi is replete with historical monuments that remind us of the splendour of the bygone dynasties. The landmark monuments dotting Delhi's urban landscape comprise of Red Fort, Jama Masjid, Humayun Tomb, Safdarjung's Tomb, Qutab Minar, Purana Qila and Jantar Mantar. Some of the other historical sights, not as conspicuous are Feroze Shah Kotla, Begumpuri Masjid which stands in the heart of Jahanpanah—the Muhammad-bin-Tughlaq's capital and the palace of Vijay Mandal. At Tughlaqabad, on the foothills of the Aravallis lies the ruins of Delhi's third city.

At Hauz Khas lies a small structure known as Chor Minar (Tower of Thieves) of the 14th Century Khilji period. Close by is the famous Nili Masjid (Blue Mosque). At Khirkee, the unusual two-storeyed Khirkee (Windows) Mosque, built by Feroze Shah Tughlaq's Prime Minister Khan-I-Juman Shah in mid-fourteenth Century is a building with innovative architecture design.*

The various Muslim dynasties left behind an imposing array of monuments and deserted cities. But it was not until the reign of Shahjahan in the Sixteenth Century, that Delhi reached the zenith. It was Shahjahan, the builder of Taj Mahal, who gave Delhi its magnificent Red Fort and Jama Masjid. After Aurangzeb's death, Mughal power waned and the British gained control over the entire country.

The British settlement established in 1690 by Job Charnock of the East India Company, was called Calcutta,

---

**Source* : Archaelogical Survey of India.

grew into the Capital of British India, and remained so from 1774 to 1911, when during the reign of George V, the British Government decided to shift the capital from Calcutta. It was at the Delhi Durbar in 1911, that King George V announced the decision to shift the seat of Government to Delhi, and to build a new city the eighth Delhi to house the capital, which took 20 years to complete, located just south of the Old City.

It is of interest to note, that while the site selection committee had recommended Saugor in now Madhya Pradesh, for locating the new capital, because of its equable climate and central location, the British Government chose Delhi in deference to the age old tradition, that "he who rules Delhi, rules India".

Walled City–Shahjahanabad

Today, we have the overcrowded walled city of Delhi, built by the Emperor Shahjahan, the greatest of the Mughal builders, in mid-Seventeenth Century. The walled-city is organic in form. Its layout looks natural rather than man-made. The streets vary in width–they are rarely straight and wind sinuously throughout the city. The city was designed around meandering pedestrian movement.

Chandni Chowk–a former imperial avenue connecting the Red Fort and the Fatehpuri Mosque, where the Mughal Emperor Shahjahan once rode at the head of his lavish cavalcade, is today a hub of bustling commercial activities, where bullock-carts, cars, bicycle-rickshaws, tongas and pedestrians plow through the congested thoroughfare. The walled city of Delhi which is a square mile in area, has very high density of population, because it contains a growing population within a defensive wall. High density has made it necessary to utilise every inch of land, leaving a minimum of open space, consequently the streets are narrow, light and air scarce and sanitary conditions precarious. To add to this, the city outside the wall had not been laid out. The pattern of streets simply grew following old trails, making the city a labyrinth. These conditions became unbearable when Delhi became the capital of independent India. Old Delhi, reflects all the poverty, congestion with as many people crammed inside its narrow precincts. The walled city, today, is in a state of decay. Its old havelis which line the side lanes (Gullis) of Chandni Chowk, are architecturally significant, but are in a state of dereliction.

Old Delhi, once the pride of the Mughals is now a shadow of its erstwhile glory. The glorious city is history now. Population explosion, rampant commercialisation, unauthorised constructions, and willful neglect by the Municipal government have brought this walled city to its present sorry state.

The degeneration began with the Partition of the Country in 1947, which brought a massive influx of refugees from Pakistan. They thronged the pavements of Chandni Chowk, Khari Bawli and Dariba Kalan and started small businesses. The entire walled city has shops on the ground floor and residences on the first floor.

Being very near to both New Delhi and Old Delhi, train station, and also to Interstate Bus Terminal, the walled city developed as a wholesale market for various commodities. Small businessmen from neighbouring towns found it convenient for purchasing the goods they required: Sarees from Chandni Chowk, Paper from Khari Bawli, Chemicals from Tilak Bazaar, Electrical goods from

Bhagirath Palace, Gold and Silver from Kucha Mahajan, Stationery from Nai Sarak, and Jewellery from Dariba Kalan and Gota from Kinari Bazaar.

Today, Old Delhi portrays the dismal picture of congestion, chaotic traffic and sub-human living conditions. Most of the walled city is a slum. It has polluting small workshops in over six hundred Katras, about 260 Kuchas, 193 Kachchi bastis and 87 Pakki bastis. Have no adequate ventilation, drainage. Power lines hang loosely overhead and cause frequent fires. Rampant commercialisation, encroachment and appalling civic conditions have rendered the walled city of Delhi uninhabitable.

Although destroyed, by its masses of inhabitants and its poverty, the walled city contains beautiful buildings, havelis, sadly maltreated by negligence and time. Its streets and lanes, teeming with everyday life, are what the great cities of orient were then. There was also the relative dignity of Civil Lines of the British Raj to its North with its great Delhi University, and its over spill of residential areas, largely refugee in origin.

New Delhi

We have the prestigious and pretentious official New Delhi, designed by the British Architect, Sir Edwin Lutyen, when the British shifted their centre of power from Calcutta to Delhi in 1911. Lutyen who loved grand gestures and classic design, eventually got to put into effect his urban design for the imperial capital in the early Twentieth Century. New Delhi is geometrical, predetermined and ordered layout of city, in sharp contrast to medieval old city of Delhi (Shahjahanabad) with its narrow winding streets.

Symbolically, an imperialistic design, the capital has a great East-West processional way–the Rajpath leading to Rai Sinha Hill on which sits the domed Rashtrapati Bhawan–earlier the Viceroy's Residence with 340 rooms on a 330 acres site. At the lowest end of Rajpath is the magnificent India Gate–a war-memorial to the heroes of World War I. The land around it–the Princes Park was allotted to Princely States such as Jaipur House, Bikaner House etc. etc. The North and South Blocks–as popularly known, house the secretariats of the Central Government, each with 1000 rooms and miles of corridors. New Delhi is indeed a picturesque synthesis of classical European and Indian Architecture. New Delhi was conceived as a garden city–the design is harmonious, with wide tree-lined avenues, circular plazas and multitude of trees of different species, lovely old bungalows and affluent residential neighbourhoods.

New Delhi, unlike the walled city, was not built slowly over the centuries, reflecting the aspirations of successive generations. The main features of the British City remain. The capital continues to wear an expression of colonial grandeur : wide, tree-lined avenues, bordered by stately white colonial residences, with large, high ceiling rooms, colonnaded verandas, and spacious gardens. New Delhi, the colonial capital, was planned for 3,200 acres and a maximum population of 65,000. The plan was basically geometric in pattern, incorporating modified hexagons, triangles, trapezoids and circles. The focal point was Vice-Regal House (now Rashtrapati Bhawan) and the Secretariat Blocks, placed on Raisina Hill. Ample provision was made for golf club and race course for the colonials. The tree-lined avenues were planned, with right-of-ways ranging from 60 feet to 300 feet in width, except for the main axis (now Rajpath) of 440 feet in width.

Unfortunately, road connections to Old Delhi and to the region were inadequately provided for. A cantonment of 10,000 acres–three times the size of New Delhi City area was planned to house the military.

Pahar Ganj was reluctantly left out of the plan for New Delhi, as was Old Delhi. Patrick Geddes (author of Cities in Evolution) work on Indian towns, it is said, gave more to civilization and to history than all the monumentality of Lutyen's masterpieces at New Delhi. Their two worlds did not meet.

Delhi occupies a site which has been repeated focus of invasion. The city's inhabitants have been exposed to an endless succession of death and destruction. Nevertheless, always there has been a Delhi rising from the onslaughts and the remains left in their wake.

Delhi today is a blend of old and new, a metropolis of great contrasts, combining a walled city and an expensive and relatively new city several times the area of the old one. There are contrasts in density of population. In the old city at close to 1000 persons per acres, whereas in New Delhi 30 persons per acre.

Today, New Delhi's bungalow area is being vandalised, to the point of losing its character and image. The famous Connaught Place, designed as a westernised shopping centre, which was then sought to be kept entirely aloof from the old ones, is today overwhelmed by tall buildings around it, with non-descript architecture. The inner circle of Connaught Place is a mess, dominated by auto-repair shops. During the British Raj, Delhi was predominantly an administrative city with less than one million inhabitants. Soon, after independence, city's population rose phenomenally, from about 7 lacs to 14 lacs in the decade (1941–51), an increase of 200 per cent.

With the end of the British Rule, in August 1947, Delhi became the capital of a sovereign Indian State. A major problem of every big city has been the migration of population from impoverished rural areas and small towns, and this problem was especially acute in Delhi. It's urban population rose from 7 lacs to 14.4 lacs people in the decade (1941–51), an increase of over 200 per cent. Delhi's growth during the early post independent period was phenomenal, since 6 lacs to 7 lacs refugees migrated from Pakistan and also due to the massive growth of government employment–from colonial law and order State to the Capital of a great country dedicated to the planned welfare State. Proliferation of foreign embassies, business houses etc. all this piled up on top of natural growth.

In its ninth rebirth Delhi has emerged as an everyday modern city with its high-rise downtown–Connaught Place, its diverse residential neighbourhoods, and sprawling suburbs. People from all walks of life have found homes in Delhi and brought with them a sense of their past. It is indeed a mini-India with diversity of religious and cultural practices, and multiple languages.

2

The Urban Explosion

Urbanisation is an essential part of our national development, toward more stable and productive economy. If well managed, urbanisation has the potential to lead to improvement in the living standards of our people. Unfortunately, there never has been a neatly defined or coherent national urban policy for India, a clear notion of what the Central Government was attempting to achieve through its intervention to local government.

Consequently, the impact of unbridled urban growth on Delhi's infrastructure, has manifested most visibly in traffic congestion, insufficient drainage and sewerage system, inadequate health and education facilities, water and power shortages, rising crime and environmental degradation, rise of urban underclass and other failures in city management. The unbridled urbanisation has resulted in more urban poverty, homelessness, unemployment and social unrest. While the urban problems in Delhi are the accumulated effects of decades of human and environmental neglect, the massive urban growth in a brief period, technological change and consumption pattern have exacerbated the situation.

Delhi, the capital of India, is the epicenter of population explosion in Northern India. Great waves of people from its rural hinterland have been converging on the metropolis, swelling its population to figures, unknown before we became an independent nation. The migration of rural population to urban Delhi, is not necessarily the result of rising productivity in agriculture or growth of labour opportunities in industry. In fact, it is the rural poverty and insecurity, that has led to the push towards Delhi. It is distress migration, with most migrants heading for the metropolitan cities, where opportunities for earning a livelihood for unskilled and illiterate workers, is far greater than in small size cities or towns.

The migrants on the one hand provide Delhi with a large reserve of cheap, manual labour. On the other hand, it has brought unprecedented social problems like shelter, infrastructure, education, public health and social order. Their impacts on the nation's capital have grown so strong that the MCD and government of NCT of Delhi can no longer ignore their presence.

Overcrowded Delhi, symbolises the dangers of runaway urbanisation. The most visible and dehumanising manifestations of this surge towards urbanisation is the large numbers of squatters living in 'shanty towns', so ubiquitous on Delhi's urban landscape. The more daunting problem centres on the emergence of a sector of the population, that has been termed an urban underclass, the poorest urban residents, alienated from the mainstream society, especially the jhuggi dwellers who live a marginal existence. Marginalisation and isolation from the nation's mainstream, have systematically separated them from the social resources, opportunities that would allow them to lift themselves from their poverty.

The inhabitants of these shanty towns live in conditions that are a true insult to human dignity. For these men, women and children poverty has become a way of life and slums in which they inhabit, increasingly have become part of Delhi's urban landscape. The poor housing conditions in which the squatters live, usually accompany other social and economic factors like, ignorance, poor nutrition and lack of medical care. Their insanitary shacks (Jhuggies) foster the spread of communicable diseases. The crowding of families into small space promotes rapid spread of infection. Cholera and gastro enteritis have assumed endemic proportions in these shanty towns, which should be of grave concern to the Public Health Department of Municipal Corporation of Delhi.

Unskilled villagers with low standards of living, unable to purchase or rent any accommodation, build shacks (Jhuggies) on any vacant land, they can lay their hands on, mostly public land from which they are rarely expelled by force. Their earning capacity is very low, and as a result of the application of their primitive rural standards to such areas, the slums appear. The squatting now occurring in Delhi is virtually without precedence in humanity's struggle for shelter. Squatting is an outcome of the surge of poor people towards Delhi in search of livelihood, and the government's inability to meet their need.

Public lands in Delhi are the most attractive sites for the squatters to build their shaks (Jhuggies) on unguarded and unused vacant lands such as land reserved for public use or development, lands held by the Indian Railways and national highway, are usually the targets. More often than not the squatters are on lands meant for essential city development projects. Nearly 80% of shanties are on

DDA's land, which are designated as development areas. In the late 1970s, DDA acquired 55000 acres. As lakhs of migrants moved to Delhi, government land became easy target for squatters.

Although the occupation of land by the squatters is illegal and tenuous, it ultimately wins legislation, when they assert a moral claim backed by the pressure of numbers and of course with the patronage of the politicians for whom the squatters are a potential vote-bank. The politician have a vested interest in perpetuating squatting in the metropolis. More migrants move into take advantage of official helplessness and acquiescence. This illegal occupation of land in the capital has assumed serious proportions.

The urban poor in Delhi are the most resourceful people. First of all they have come to Delhi for a better life. The urban poor living in shanty towns, work together in highly ingenius ways. Their strategies to earn livelihoods and build shelters enable them to survive and climb out of poverty slowly.

Since the poor make effort to solve their problems of livelihood and housing, they surely need to have the means to increase their incomes and assets. Strategies designed to help the poor increase their economic strength, need to be at the centre of urban planning. If the poor have economic security, they will send their children to school, they will be able to use their increased incomes to build better shelters.

The poor living in slums have vested interest in seeing that improvements are made to their habitat. Most improvements have been made by the poor helping themselves, using income from a host of economic activities, mostly in the informal sector they are engaged in. The focus, therefore, must be on investing in the urban poor by encouraging their economic activities and by building the capacities and capital of the financial and community organisations that provide services to the most enterprising urban poor.

Whether the policy is to prevent, control, contain, direct or assist squatting, depending on the situation, we need a policy. A policy vacuum is certainly precipitating or even accelerating squatting and to the presently gathering chaos, with all its political and social byproducts.

The problem of shelter for the urban poor in the capital has to be tackled in relation to broader issues of urban development. Poor shelter, as poor nutrition, poor health and poor education is a consequence of poverty. Strategies directed towards enabling the poor to help themselves will be ineffective if they do not address the causes of poverty.

It follows then, that strategies oriented towards improving housing conditions of the urban poor cannot be divorced from strategies aimed at creating employment opportunities. The migrants moving into Delhi from the villages are uneducated and unskilled, which makes them unemployable. The challenge posed by the inter-related problems of shelter and unemployment is truly one of historical dimensions. Whether or not our country is able to meet it will have a profound bearing, not only on the well-being and welfare of the millions of poor living in cities, but also on the future of the nation.

Getting jobs in the formal sector is beyond the reach of the poor, since they require literacy, skill and experience, and a level of training, which the poor find difficult to acquire. Therefore, the informal sector is a critical component in urban employment. Urban informal sector accounts for a high proportion of the urban workforce in Delhi. It absorbs those who cannot find productive employment in rural areas or in formal urban activities. However, very little is being done to promote this sector because of government's indifference, consequently employment opportunities for the poor are reduced. A realistic strategy must place major emphasis on increasing the earning opportunities of the urban poor in the informal sector, which has become an integral part of the urban economy and a positive contributor to economic growth. Government should assist the small producer and self-employed, because the entrepreneur is an important factor in the economic system, irrespective of whether he operates in informal or formal sector. The informal sector, which provides livelihood to the urban poor, is the entry level into the urban economy and indeed the national economy. Functioning of the informal sector should be facilitated, because urban productivity cannot be increased without increasing the productivity of the urban informal sector. Urban informal sector provides jobs and income for the working poor.

Government intervention and support is absolutely essential to assist the urban poor in increasing their productivity and earning opportunities. The fundamental consideration underlying such a programme is of reassessment of the role of Delhi as a city in the development process. Municipal government in Delhi has limited powers and resources at its disposal to address the employment problem.

The people living in poverty in the jhuggis must get the benefits of economic reforms. The economic change must reach ordinary people of Delhi. It must result in a visible improvement in the standard of living of these overwhelming majority of Delhi's residents. This means liberalization must produce jobs for these unemployed and underemployed. The market per se does not hold any magic for those who cannot afford to enter the marketplace.

The urban poor living in Delhi's Jhuggis are beginning to see the possibilities for a better life, the political and economic freedom now offers them. Liberalisation should liberate the creative energies of these people, involving them in the grand adventure that development can become. For it will have the effect, not merely of producing growth and prosperity, but of giving them a psychological stake in new India, an India that they see as serving their needs. So far the economic reforms have only helped the rich. Youth and students without economic prospects are ready material for violence and militancy.

The Delhi metropolis shows sizable quarters, which have preserved their rural character, especially in shanty towns and villages that have been engulfed by urbanisation. Here, the life is carried on under general conditions, only little different from those of the 'rural village'. This is reflected in the life-style and attitudes of that part of the city-people, which has not broken their ties with village-life and is only partially and incompletely urbanised. The squatter settlements are without running water, drainage and indoor plumbing, and wood smoke from cooking fires fills the air and raw sewage runs through its narrow unpaved lanes are a common sight.

Thus, the cultural impact of the metropolis, in the process of modernization is exerted upon a people who are culturally and psychologically farther removed from accepting change. These are the 'non-committed' urbanites. The rural migrants to Delhi only contribute to swelling of numbers in urban population, through a process of numerical urbanisation, without the commensurate increase in urban productivity. Delhi, like her sister cities is a mere human agglomeration that is anti-city in character. The employment and under employment among migrants from rural areas make overhead requirements more costly per capita.

Delhi's urban growth, thus, is accompanied by low levels of income, net savings and skewed income distribution, plus high costs associated with infrastructure, housing and urban services, which are the critical factors contributing to the deteriorating urban environment. The rapid population growth in Delhi cannot, therefore, be considered as growing markets, as majority of the new arrivals are among the poorest people and unskilled, and because they are prevented from meaningful participation in the market place or in development they cannot provide skilled labour, cannot buy or sell valuable goods or valuable labour. Notwithstanding the promise of the city, no matter how unlikely to be fulfilled, is more attractive than the abject poverty of the village.

A simplistic business view is that growing population in cities means growing markets. However, this is so only where needs are being converted into markets. In our country needs remain needs, and the poorest in their millions remain largely outside nation's political and economic systems, and outside any but, most basic, usually the informal markets.

Persistent poverty is ultimately one of the mechanisms of a 'free-market', where people at the top of the stratification enjoy extreme prosperity, many more just get by, while the majority find themselves the victims of an economy that has failed them. So, a balance must be struck. Shanty towns in Delhi are not viable communities. They cannot support their inhabitants. Its businesses are geared towards satisfaction of personal needs and are marginal to the economy of Delhi as a whole. The shanty town dwellers feed upon themselves, they do not produce goods or contribute to the prosperity of the metropolis.

Rehabilitation projects of the DDA designed to clean up or relocate the shanty towns have repeatedly failed, turning into worse then the slums they replaced. We need measures that will enable the squatter population to climb out of poverty. Poverty has to be fought on the battle field of economics. Empowering the urban poor to help themselves by creating a just society, this must be made a top priority on Central and Government of the NCT of Delhi agenda.

The cause of poverty in our country dates back to the Imperial Rule, when the British enacted 'land settlement act' which vested land ownership to the Zamindars (landlords) created to maintain rural order gave rise to landless peasantry. The lower class landless peasantry in the villages were so oriented to day-to-day living, that they attached no value to work, self-improvement, or service to family or community.

This behaviour and attitude needs to be changed by instilling in these poor rural migrants who have come to the city a sense of self-worth and the ability to pursue their aspirations relatively free of unwanted masters. Persistent poverty undermines the spirit and strength of our nation. The ultimate challenge is not just to manage the symptoms of poverty, but to change the social arrangements that perpetuate it.

Addressing widespread and persistent poverty amongst over one-third of the population of Delhi Metropolis is hardly a matter to be left to government alone. In fact it is an issue central to businesses. Businesses realise that the broader the base of skilled and talented workers and prosperous consumers, the greater their own rewards. Crucial part of poverty eradication is the creating of wealth, which is best left to entrepreneurs and businesses.

In Delhi, the rich minority and the poor majority share the same territory. A divided city could never be prosperous. Therefore, we have to take steps to reduce economic inequality. The urban poor are beginning to see the possibilities for a better life the political and economic freedom now offers them. Ultimately, it is the freedom offered each individual that creates economic wealth. Economies are built from the ground up by individuals devising ways to earn a living.

The challenge of our hard-earned democracy is of meeting the basic material needs of all Indians. Economic policies, therefore, are central to political prospects. The urban poor must reap the benefits of economic reforms. The economic change must reach the poor. It must result in a visible improvement in their standards of living. Liberalisation must produce jobs for the unemployed. The free market holds no magic for the poor who cannot afford to enter the market place. With a soaring number of middle-class the government may be encouraged to believe in its economic reforms ; but accompanying this increase in middle-class is the disparity of wealth.

Economic Impact of Squatter on Delhi

To be able to show the government and the public, that it cannot afford not to solve the squatter problem, studies need to be initiated to quantify the economic impact of squatters on the metropolis. Unless one can describe a phenomenon using numbers, one knows very little about it, writes Rene Descartes. Nevertheless, economic impact of squatters, go much deeper into the fabric of the metropolis, than the rupee figures, the studies may indicate. For in quantifying the impact of squatters, numbers cannot be attached to the deepest impacts—the moral and societal damage done by growing presence of squatters in the national capital.

How does one put a number, on the brutalisation of the squatters, living in filth and squalor of slums, or the brutalisation of the society increasingly inured to their presence, or on the moral damage done to our younger people, who see that society seems incapable or unwilling of living up to its most basic responsibilities. Who can assess the cost of the loss to our future, because children in the shanty towns are being deprived of the educational skills that would make them contributing members. But unfortunately people's attention is drawn only when their pocketbooks are threatened. To get the attention of the people, the direct impact of squatters on the tax payers needs to be demonstrated.

Squatters as an economic problem is costing the metropolis in lakhs of rupees in lost tax revenues, risk of epidemics, risk of major fires, loss of labour and capital, social services, rehousing, and occupation of prime land in the capital. The costs to society of people living in poverty are enormous. Reducing poverty can thus greatly ease the tax burden for all.

Investments in the development of the workforce should be well-supported, especially given the importance of reducing poverty levels. We should not underestimate human beings' capacity for self-improvement, and we can't afford to do so. The grave problems of the urban underclass and the resulting disintegration of city life in our time can be viewed as the failure of a particular species of political idealism. The government is supposed to promote the supply of jobs and also the training for these jobs. The poor may live in cramped shacks in shanty towns, but they have access to parks, low-cost public transit, free public schools and health facilities.

The urban underclass must cease to be an underclass and become a working class of honourably occupied people, who make less money, but share the city with others and observe the same standard of public conduct as everybody else. They may live in less desirable houses, but they need not live in squalor. They can share the aspirations of the main stream and they can exercise their will to move upward in society by the traditional means of education, diligence, and respectful behaviour. Break the hold on individuals of those aspects of the jhuggi culture that work against upward mobility, by providing a constant, powerful force that encourages the people of the jhuggis to consider themselves part of the social structure of the city as a whole.

Task Force on Squatter Settlements

"If a free society cannot help the many who are poor, it cannot save the few who are rich". –*John F. Kennedy*

Squatters a grave national problem, is receiving remarkably scant attention. The indifferent attitude of the authorities regard for the issue of squatters—urban poor is appalling. The problem of poverty and unemployment are deeply entrenched. 'Quick-fix' policies blind us to real solutions, such as fully funding education and providing jobs that pay a wage that can support a family.

It is important, that our perception of who the poor and homeless are, catches up to reality, because there are warning signs that time is running out. With a soaring number of middle class–our government may be encouraged to believe in its economic reforms, but accompanying this increase in middle class has been a disparity of wealth.

Despite numerous social programmes designed to alleviate the sufferings of the poor, more people now live in poverty than before. We must understand the gravity of the situation–poverty and homelessness are not situations we can afford to ignore, or dismiss as a minor problem or blame on the poor themselves because of their perceived laziness. The programmes that can significantly help the poor are : Healthcare, education, manpower training, safe drinking water, low cost housing.

It is time for us to re-examine the unfulfilled promises of 'Garibi Hatao'. We need to review several programmes, policies and strategies for managing or ending poverty, that government has introduced since independence in the last fifty years. Empowering the urban poor to help themselves, by creating a just society, must be made a top priority on the Government of NCT of Delhi Agenda. Need to examine the process by which the State/MCD might assess squatter situation and how it might go about creating a blue print for action that is something more than a gut response to somebody else's distress.

Unfortunately, the politicians in Delhi perceive their own political interest to be served best, by the persistence of squatter settlement, and they quietly act to assure that persistence, because squatters are their vote banks. Delhi's political leadership, as well as the community leadership, must decide soon to face up to the squatter problem, and organise itself to do something about it. Actions generally cannot wait until we have all the answers. No task force set up to address the problem of shanty towns, should allow itself to become an excuse for delay in taking obviously needed actions.

Economic reforms have spawned a small but all-too visible class of supper rich in the nation's capital, while the underclass is slipping farther from the mainstream. Liberalisation should liberate and fulfill the creative energies of our people, involving them in the development process.

As long as a permanent underclass and permanent unemployment exist on the present scale in Delhi, fundamental urban problems will remain. For whatever we may do about rebuilding Delhi, won't matter without more long-term productivity jobs, for the minimally educated and minimally skilled. Recognition of this basic economic reality underscores the urgency of redirecting urban development strategies and priorities.

Poverty in the national capital, most visible in shanty towns and slum areas, cannot be eliminated by urban design, it has to be fought on the economic battlefield. More and more people in Delhi must get the benefit of India's economic reforms. The economic change we experience today, must reach the ordinary citizen. It must result in a visible improvement, in the standard of living of the overwhelming majority of people, including the poor. This means liberalisation must produce jobs for the city's unemployed or underemployed. Life, liberty and pursuit of happiness are inconceivable, without the opportunity to earn a decent livelihood, secure life's basic necessities, and contribute to society. We need to do a revaluation of the conditions of our less fortunate inhabitants of Delhi who are the victims of poverty and homelessness.

The Government of the National Capital Territory of Delhi must develop the jobs suitable for a critical portion of its population. A distinction must be made between different pools of labour. For instance, those engaged in short-term construction jobs and those engaged in long-term production and service jobs.

Millions in Delhi are competing in the global economy driven and defined by the computer age, but we should not forget millions of urban poor, who are left behind, unable to compete in the global world. The Jhuggi dwellers unable to earn enough to keep up with the standards of rest of the people have to be helped. They will require more than one generation of help, until their earning ability lets them have a chance in free enterprise.

We as a nation have neglected education in a truly regrettable way. Countries threatened by globalisation are those, where human development was very low. The success stories in Asia are built on the twin foundation of higher productivity and a greater concern for equity and investment in human capital.

Americans, for example, were well positioned for economy-building, by virtue of their sense of self-worth and their ability to pursue their dreams and aspirations relatively free of unwanted masters. We too need to extend a sense of individuality and self-worth to that section of our population that has become so dependent on the government.

Education is a powerful weapon in the fight against poverty. The urban poor must be provided with skills they need to participate in a more competitive market economy. Providing access to education is the first great step toward breaking the cycle of poverty and improving the standard of living. We need to transform the people living in shanty towns into an economic resource. We know that literally hundreds and thousands of families, men, women and children, the perfectly okay and the employable, the old and the young, are without adequate education, training and shelter. It is an enduring shame for the society, and we continue to allow it.

One of the best ways to fight poverty, and encourage economic growth, is to educate girls and women. Educating girls is one of the most effective ways to achieve significant and long-lasting social and economic benefits for poor families and communities. Families have traditionally viewed school attendance as unimportant, and as hindering girls from carrying out household chores. In our country, the debilitating cycle of poverty has a gender bias. Too often, female children and adolescents bear the brunt of the family's deprivation by dropping out of school early, to shoulder domestic responsibilities, including care for younger siblings. These girls have little choice when both parents need to work to support the family. As a result, the girl's childhood is lost and her development stunted, sentencing her to a life of limited possibilities. The problems exacerbates itself. Due to fatigue, malnutrition or illness, the girl's performance at school is poor. Parents assume the child lacks interest or is not making any efforts at school and, since her help is so necessary at home, the decision is made for her to drop out.

The Government of NCT of Delhi must start a programme involving female children and teenagers from shanty towns, to provide them with opportunities to overcome education, health and recreational disadvantages. The activities should be planned and organised with the participation of the girls' mothers, who should be elected to committees that also manage programmes' funds. The Government of NCT of Delhi should set up education support centres for providing educational support for girls with learning problems as well as offering educational workshops, covering such topics as organisation, study techniques, hygiene and self-esteem. The integrated coverage must be designed to stimulate the girls' personal and educational growth and develop both cognitive and social skills.

There is a need for national policy to encourage the States, Cities and private agencies to provide, especially for low income groups and economically weaker sections, adequate recreational and cultural opportunities for personal self-development, free-self-expression, and group participation in plays, art, literature, science and education for youth and adults. The Central Government should further these aims by cooperating with and giving financial aid to, the Government of NCT of Delhi and other public and private agencies, in their efforts, thus, to raise the level of life in the nation's capital.

However, any solution for poverty and related problems in Delhi will be short-term unless, at the same time, it can stem rural to urban migration by improving living conditions and employment opportunities in small cities and large villages.

Job Training

It is impossible to think of urban poverty in all its dimensions, without thinking of education, because if you had an education, you probably wouldn't be in poverty. Most of the squatters barely scrape out an existence in odd jobs and self-employment. These are the people who live in generational poverty, who have been indigent for generations in time immemorial. They live surrounded by myriad social problems, such as poor educational opportunities, caste abuse etc. Those in generational poverty do not grow up in a culture of work. The challenge of helping them enter the workforce regimes intensive public investment in training programmes that will give them the marketable skills they need. Introduce marketable job training programmes.

The Government of the NCT of Delhi must introduce job training programmes to prepare State's Citizens for the job of the future. Under this programme the State MLAs should get out into their constituencies and initiate contact between State Officials and the citizens. This programme will afford average person an opportunity to be heard and bring the State Government closer to the people.

The Government of the NCT of Delhi must set up Joint Committee on Labour, for better understanding of the labour needs of business and industry and the training and retaining needs of workers, hold meeting around the State. The MLAs should visit job training sites and learn from their training experiences and programmes. In conjunction with these visits, the MLAs should hold public forums and listen to business, labour, educators and the general public voice their opinions on the State's job needs and training programmes.

MLAs responsibility is not merely to attend assembly sessions. They must establish a comprehensive labour market information system to reflect the State's overall training and education efforts.

The major components of the system should be :

1. To provide citizens training opportunities ;
2. Objective, fact-based performance information, on workforce development programme, service and activities ; and
3. Projection on workforce growth, job growth and demand State and region-wise.

The State Government must assist students exploring careers, adults seeking re-training and the unemployed pursuing employment. Central and State Governments should make available financial aid for local job-training and job placement.

Millions of children are out of school, trying to scratch out a living, doing everything from begging with their mothers to working in hazardous industries. Education will increasingly be the factor that distinguishes "haves" from "have-nots". Education is the key to break the cycle of poverty. NGOs must operate job-training programmes for jhuggi dwellers and homeless ; helping them improve their skills and return to the mainstream of society–that is a stable living situation, steady employment, and a manageable life.

Housing–Urban Poor

"The strength of a nation is in the intelligent and well-ordered homes of the people." —*Lydia Sigonrney.*

There is an acute shortage of affordable housing in Delhi. This is evident from the increasing numbers of homeless people. Regardless of one's attitude towards these unfortunate people, the problem of homelessness is increasingly everyone's problem. Lack of adequate shelter and employment opportunities for the urban poor, results in disrupted family life, 'street children', social alienation, learning disabilities, crime and violence. Slum dwellers say, we spent our lives on the pavement and in jhuggis, we do not want our children to do that. The concerned authorities in Delhi are losing sight of the gravity of this Capital's housing problem.

Housing the poor has become an especially salient issue, in the wake of low real income growth and rising housing costs. The poor do not live in adequate housing. In fact three million live in housing deemed inadequate.

The crisis of homelessness was recognised as one of the world's most pressing social problems when the UN declared 1987 to be the International Year of Shelter. Poor people simply cannot afford housing. They are priced out of the housing market. Over three million people in Delhi lie in 'life-and-health-threatening' homes in Jhugiis, because of poor shelter and living conditions, and the lack of adequate provision for sanitation, drainage, removal of garbage and health care. It's a form of social oppression.

The inability to make or to earn enough income to rent or buy a house, alongwith the lack of resources to meet food, clothing and medical needs, impacts, both the physical quality of life and emotional well-being of families. We have to find ways and means of providing a decent-home and a suitable living environment for every family in the shanty towns. The search for affordable housing represents an ever-growing challenge for the government.

The squatter settlements numbering about a thousand with a total population of over 3 million–did not come into being overnight, and it will not be solved instantly either. The longest journey begins with a single step and as light is shed, denial becomes impossible. What is lacking is the political commitment, particularly from our local officials, to restrain or steer housing market forces to benefit poor and working class people of Delhi. Housing should be made an issue in local politics.

No intelligent urban strategy can overlook the facts, that millions of jhuggi dwellers in the national capital already live in misery, filth and neglect. Their problems are not going to go away. They are very much there, the squatters are there, and their numbers keep growing. Government is not able to provide them with shelter, services or income sources. The problems of urban poverty can be resolved by the poor people themselves with backing from NGOs and other social welfare organisations.

The urban poor are perhaps the most resourceful people, who have come to Delhi to make a better life. Their relentless effort to earn livelihood and build shelters enables them to survive. If these poor people living in Jhuggis are solving their own problems of employment and shelter, they need the means to increase their incomes. Strategies aimed to assist them in increasing their economic strength and security need to be at the centre of urban planning in the national capital. The non-government organisations, should initiate programmes, wherein the jhuggi dwellers and homeless help build their own houses, with technical and financial assistance from the government.

Poor are good at constructing their own houses. Housing provided by government is expensive, and insensitive to the needs of the poor. We must unleash the productive forces of the urban poor, and forge a partnership. What the poor have to put into the partnership is essentially their labour. There are technical and other problems, which the poor cannot solve by themselves. It is here, that the architectural profession in Delhi can make a major contribution. The architect can guide what is essentially a self-reliant or self-help project. Using his professional skills, the architect can help the poor to a cheap solution of the problem of roofing, which is the most difficult building problem.

We need persons of exceptional leadership ability, to inspire and motivate others to become involved in the issues of housing the poor. Forging partnerships in which government, private non-profit organisations and communities join forces to improve opportunities for the urban poor. Central Government should lead efforts to improve living conditions in the shanty towns, because only it can undertake such an enormous task. The idea is to bring the urban poor into the mainstream of society. The State and local city governments would follow the Central Government's lead, and create their own social programmes once shanty town improvements were shown to be effective.

We should try to bring the jhuggi dwellers closer to the social and economic mainstream of Indian society, and not encouraging them to develop a self-contained community apart from the mainstream. Slum-dwellers should form a federation, to strengthen local savings and credit schemes, and to lobby for greater cooperation with the authorities. Such federations have a big impact on slum upgrading schemes around the world. Women's group should organise slum dwellers/jhuggi dwellers into savings club that allows them to borrow small amounts of money to start shorts or repair homes.

Rent Control

Rent controls are introduced to serve a basic public purpose–the protection of tenants from unfair rent increase. Rent control is a pure price control, and price controls invariably produce commodity shortages–housing shortages.

Rent control introduced in Delhi, has often been criticised, because it induces tenants to live in the same houses for many years, thereby reducing the availability of houses and creating housing shortages in the city. Although such rent control policy helps low-income tenants, who stay in the same house for many years, its principal long-term effect is to reduce the profitability of rental housing and thus putting the burden of providing housing for low-income groups on government. While rent control favours existing tenants in Delhi by holding down their rents, at the same time it reduces the availability of housing to all other prospective tenants. It also raises the rent of houses which are outside the purview of rent control act. Rent control deters investments in either maintenance or new construction. It really makes it hard for investors to build or renovate.

Rent control is a counter productive measure. Because no system of rent control can ensure the availability of decent and affordable housing for low, and moderate income families in Delhi. Whether or not rents are regulated, more direct remedies are required, including programmes that supplement the rents that low and moderate income tenants can afford to pay ; that preserve existing low-rent housing and ; that induce the production of additional low and moderate cost rental housing.

Rent control is a recipe for a permanent crisis, because by suppressing the return on landlord's investments, it discourages the construction of new units. Rent control discourages home ownership. Rent control also discourages upkeeping of existing dwelling units. The bottom line is rent control puts the landlord class out of the business of creating housing opportunities. Rent control has drastically reduced incentives for private investment in affordable rental housing. As a result, Delhi finds itself lacking both inadequate supply of affordable housing and a mechanism for ensuring affordability over the long run. Recognising need for affordable rental housing ; in order to meet the bloated demand, we should establish housing programmes. Programme must offer private-sector economic incentives to invest in affordable housing to supplement government subsidies. A decreasing rate of private housing, combined with unprecedented increases in rents and housing prices, has made it difficult for low-income working families to find houses in Delhi.

Government of NCT of Delhi must decide to make affordable housing a major policy objective. It has to address the affordable housing crisis by encouraging increased housing development. Create a partnership between private housing developers and local government (Housing Authority). Motivate local government in Delhi, to work with private and non-profit sectors, to develop affordable housing, and to provide technical and financial assistance to facilitate such initiatives. Economic incentives are a powerful means of encouraging participation in a programme, like economic incentives to developers to concentrate on developing low-income housing. Tax exemptions to organisations or individuals to invest in a fund that supports the development of low-cost housing. The Central Government must look into the possibility of establishing a housing trust fund, to provide the capital needed to produce affordable housing.

3

This is Your City–Delhi

The Delhi of today is the capital of the sovereign State of India. In its present state it is infact, an amorphous mass of built area, which proliferates and expand promiscuously, destroying the surrounding landscape, while leaving large internal areas of deterioration. Metropolitan Delhi is a pan-urban region, a conglomeration of cities, suburbs and urban villages, loosely set together, quite separate in character, origin and to a great extent in function, Delhi has grown with multiple urban cores. Delhi metropolis is shaped not only by planners, but also by the often idiosyncratic decision of large numbers of separate citizens and builders and developers.

An unceasing influx of business and people, is changing the tenor and character of Delhi. From a stodgy government city, the national capital has turned into a thriving business centre with startups and multi-national companies, thronging in. Between 1991 and 2000, Delhi's population increased by 43 per cent, which is faster than any other city in India, and today it has a population of over 15 million people. In another decade 6 million people will be added. Between 1981 and 1991, 50 per cent of the population growth was due to migration from UP, Haryana, Rajasthan, Punjab and Bihar. About a million people come daily to the Capital from adjacent urban settlements in Haryana and Uttar Pradesh.

Many multi-national companies have chosen Delhi as their base. Industrial units employ over a million workers, and there are over half million government employees. In the past few years the jobs in the metropolis have grown at least twice as fast as in Mumbai. Delhi is nation's most affluent market, an average family earns Rs. 21,830 per year against the national average of Rs. 9,321. Delhiites spend larger portion of their income on consumption, than their counterparts in other parts of the country.

Metropolitan cities are the engines that drive India's economy. Delhi metropolis contributes substantially to the Gross National Product (GNP). The political power base of Delhi, coupled with its economic importance creates an opportunity to develop a fresh approach to urban management system capable of optimising both social and economic development.

While there are illusions that the national capital gives impression of prosperity, yet in reality nearly half the population lives in abject poverty, squalor and degradation, where human values are ruthlessly debased under appalling and humiliating living conditions.

So many different images are conjured up in the vast metropolis of Delhi. Rural migrants in shanty towns, crowded streets and marketplaces, encroachments on sidewalks and street curbs, hawkers, pushcarts, stray dogs and cattle, slums, crowded tenements, filth and squalor and dangerous small scale industries, and traffic-gridlocks.

There are parts of Delhi metropolis that can hardly be called urban. The streets are pot holed dirt-roads, through which spill a mixture of raw-sewage and garbage. The people in jhuggiis continue to defecate on the wayside as they did in their villages. It's a cultural problem, since they are accustomed to doing these things in their villages.

The bazaars (market), through which countless people pass, many times each day, are chaotic, dirty and disease prone. Bazaars are congested, their open drains are often choked with garbage and filth, and dirty water flows in all directions. People urinate and defecate near drains adjacent to the shops. In general appearance, bazaars in the capital are unattractive and need much improvement. Articles and food are dumped indiscriminately, food handlers display an amazing disregard for sanitary and hygienic principles. Signboards are haphazardly erected. Extensive and unauthorised encroachments on the pavements are chronic features of any bazaar or market.

In a large metropolitan city like Delhi, people exhibit far more anti-social behaviour, hostility, and selfishness, than its counterparts in medium and small towns. The national capital is composed of heterogeneous population, full of impersonal human beings, living in clusters of regional ethnic, communities without a sense of emotional integration. They are made up of strata of unequal groups, which are often exclusive, competitive and mutually exploitative. Delhi is a mixture of magnificence, and of squalor, of bungalows and shacks, of great opportunity for some and despondency for many. It is alien to the cultural experiences of most of its inhabitants, who came from the villages.

It shows sizeable quarters, which have preserved their rural character, especially among the economically-weaker section of the population living in slums and shanty-towns, where life is carried on under general conditions, only little different from that of the village. This in turn is reflected in the life-style and attitudes of that part of the population, which has not broken their ties with village life and are only partially and incompletely urbanised. The cultural impact of the metropolis in the process of modernisation is exerted upon a people, who are actually and psychologically, farther removed from accepting change. These are the non-committed urbanites.

The nation's capital faces a dilemma. On the one hand, unskilled migrants who are drawn to Delhi metropolis occupy public land, put demands on civic services, but contribute nothing to the Municipal revenues. On the other hand, the economic prosperity has led to the emergence of a relatively affluent middle-class, which makes even more demands on the city services, without contributing commensurately to the Municipal revenues. Indeed, it is this class that puts pressure on housing demands, that are often met by developers and builders. The windfall profit made from intensive use of urban real estate goes to the builder, whereas the unbearable burden of maintaining the civic services or augmenting them falls on the Municipal Corporation of Delhi. Is it not ironical that the real estate developers and builders garner huge profits from city's land resources, while the Municipal Coffers remain depleted to the extent that it is unable even the maintenance of existing infrastructure facilities and services.

The cost of operating and maintaining the national capital is far greater than the city government can afford. The achievement of decent living conditions for the large number of residents in this vast and rapidly growing metropolis is extremely difficult and costly, probably impossible at least for now. It may be much easier and cheaper to ensure gradual progress in living conditions in medium and smaller towns around Delhi. There seems to be no valid reason why basic economic progress requires metropolitan concentration as a general pattern. However, this is not to imply that Delhi metropolis is to be abandoned or that it is not possible to arrest its further growth entirely, but that the present trend towards over centralisation needs to be abated.

The Delhi metropolis must be contained, because it plays a dominant role in National Capital Region in which it is located. Whether we support decentralisation or centralisation theory, the fact remains that India has a great commitment to its metropolitan cities which are the engines of economic growth and contribute in large measure to the GNP. Hence, the country cannot turn its back to the needs of the Capital.

The success or failure of the city to create jobs, provide affordable housing, and maintain the environment, is the measure of our success or failure as a nation. Therefore, it is very much in the national interest for the Central Government to assist the nation's capital in carrying out broad national policy goals and in its efforts as incubators and sustainers of economic growth.

Delhi metropolis has been allowed to grow and expand without any control regardless of elementary human needs of its inhabitants, until it has become virtually unmanageable today. The unbridled expansion of Delhi metropolis is self-defeating, because with every new increment of population, its traffic becomes more congested, its central institution less accessible and the larger parts of its population are as little benefited, by its higher institutions of culture, as if they were entirely outside its orbit.

In 1951, four years after India became an independent nation the population of Delhi was 17.44 lakh people. Delhi's population has been growing by more than 50 per cent growth rate in each successive census since 1951. At that rate, by 1991 Delhi's population rose to 94.20 lakh people, and at present it is 150 lakhs. With the increase in population, Delhi's urban area also expanded to 685.34 square kilometers.

Delhi with its vast impoverished hinterland attracts a very large migrant population. In fact, the migrant population constitutes about two-fifths of Delhi's urban population. The net migration to Delhi, which was 13 lakhs during the decade 1981-91, is expected to increase to 24 lakhs during the decade 2011-2021.* Most of these migrants land up in squatter settlements. They constitute 35 per cent of the total urban population of Delhi.

The migration pattern indicates, highest number of migrants comes from impoverished areas of Uttar Pradesh (about 50 cent). Rest are from Bihar, Haryana, Rajasthan and the Punjab. It is the employment opportunities in Delhi that generates migration. The migrant population constitutes 56 per cent of workers who are mostly employed in bluecollar jobs. To certain extent, migrants determine Delhi's nature of economic activity.

Delhi also has a large day time population. About 20 lakh intercity trips per day are made by persons coming from outside Delhi. These commuters visit the national

---

**Source:* Directorate of Economic and Statistics. Government of NCT of Delhi.

capital daily for employment, education, health and other purposes.

Delhi, a large and spread out metropolis requires huge energy inputs to remain viable. High energy consumption in turn causes ecological changes for instance intensive use of fossil fuel leads to heating up of the atmosphere, due to emission from over 2 million air-conditioners and solar reflection caused by network of streets and hundreds of tall buildings.

Because of its ungovernable traffic, Delhi has become the world's fourth most polluted metropolis. Motor vehicles in Delhi spew 1,430 tons of exhaust fumes into the atmosphere daily, enough to ring the inside of your nose, with slack carbon within moments of leaving the house. On an average a Delhiites inhales the toxic equivalent of the smoke of 20 cigarettes daily. About 7,500 people die from pollution related diseases each year. Four million people are treated for them at capital's hospitals.

The cost of providing adequate capacity to our urban highways add the expense of building many extra kilometers of water and sewer lines, electricity lines, and other infrastructure to serve the sprawling metropolitan Delhi.

Intra-city transportation costs are higher because of street congestion. Congestion diseconomies of urban scale, such as lengthy and costly daily journeys-to-work and central area traffic jams, is yet another dilemma. Added to that are the human cost manifested in the physical and mental agony of the day-to-day travel in the overcrowded buses. If one computes the value of the man-hours lost in urban travel, the human energy and fuel spent, it would show that any such metropolis in India turns extremely unproductive after exceeding the limit of growth—the urban threshold. After a certain level the social costs far outweigh the economies of scale Delhi Metropolis enjoys, which have never been reckoned in evaluating the role of laissez-faire urban policies in the process of India's economic development.

In an age, when globalization and new technology are bringing hitherto unimaginable benefits to one part of our society in Delhi, it is shameful and unacceptable that another part, a larger part, remains excluded from these benefits. Behind this blinding glitter of the new millionaires, Delhi is failing bulk of its inhabitants.

After more than decade of free-market reforms, both poverty and economic inequality have risen in Delhi. Privatization largely spawned a new generation of billionaires, while earnings of most of the people remains static or worsened. Today, about 40 per cent of Delhi's population lives below poverty line, earning less than Rs. 1,250 per month.

A symptom of this malady is the spiraling crime rate in the capital, because the have-nots seem to take matters into their own hands. It is their way of focusing government's attention on the plight of those who are left out of the economic prosperity of the time—the urban poor are beginning to see the possibilities for a better life.

There is a shocking contrast of poverty and wealth in the nation's capital, which has begun to breed bitterness and frustration among the underprivileged majority. Delhi, like other metropolitan cities of India, is virtually exclusive home of the most troubling aspect of our poverty problem, and metropolitanism is further aggravating

India's drift towards the conditions of a polarised dual society.

As one moves around so many different images conjure up on Delhi's urban landscape–Shanty towns (jhuggis), pavement dwellers, street-children, vagabonds loitering around in shopping centres, hawkers, stray cattle, littered garbage, open drains, persons defecating on wayside, encroachments along street etc.

Congestion in Delhi is so conspicuous in every phase of the city's life. One sees congestion in the constant stoppage of vehicular traffic on the roads. One encounters congestion at railway stations, in the buses, at shopping centres and bazaars, in hospitals, school rooms and housing.

Delhi has grown to giant size, exploded by new technologies beyond recognition, beyond an ability to function well, beyond the ability of citizens to control the forces that shaped everyday life. Political leaders and businessmen had grown indifferent to the consequences, to the hard living conditions of the metropolis.

- How fully does the national capital expresses the principles of health, freedom, equality, and security which we believe in? How closely does it reflect our scientific ability and technical knowledge? How worthy is our national capital of the term "Civilization"?

- Most of the citizens know that what is happening in the capital is one of the most serious urban crisis of our time. Yet there is nothing resembling a national commitment, let alone a national strategy to do anything about it. Delhi with declining resources, is essentially left to fend for itself against growing odds. The consequences of neglect are growing worse. The longer we ignore the problems, the harder and more expensive it will be to solve them.

- Urban planners need to address questions such as–how large can an urban area grow before it loses coherence and efficiency? Which design best embodies modern techniques of transportation? What is the proper relationship between the central city and its region.

Water Supply

Delhi faces a shortage of about 200 mgd of water. 42 per cent to 45 per cent of available water is lost in pilferage, leaks, seepage. The decades-old water lines have got corroded and most of them have got mixed with sewage lines. Water is one of the more vital natural resources and one of the basic elements for life. Therefore, it is incumbent on part of the city government to provide potable water supply to all the citizens of Delhi. The water supply should be available at all times and in such quantities as will provide for all the personal and household uses and for the disposal of waste substances from the dwelling units.

The amount of water required to maintain a desirable level of sanitation, comfort and cleanliness depends on many factors, such as climate, the socio-economic conditions and customs. In large urbanised area, like the Delhi Metropolis, 270 litres per person per day is suggested by the WHO as the minimum amount of water that needs to be supplied for domestic purposes only.

Urban Threshold

The chronic shortage of water supply in Delhi should be a pointer to limiting urban expansion. With limited supply from the Yamuna River, people in Delhi resort to tubewell water thereby lowering the water table to dangerous levels. Tapping water from a distance source would entail miles of pipeline and a number of reservoirs. Each additional mile of pipeline and each additional reservoir adds to the unit cost.

Disposal of Sewage and Liquids, Solid Wastes

The disposal of sewage and liquid and solid wastes is a major public health problem. It is important not only from the aesthetic viewpoint, but also because sewage and waste materials may contain pathogenic organisms, which are easily transmitted by direct contamination or by water, food, insects or rodents.

When garbage is not collected and disposed of in a sanitary manner, it gives rise to an insect or rodent infestation. City lacks an efficient garbage collection and disposal system. Trash is littered all over the streets from garbage dumps.

45 per cent of Delhi lacks a proper sewage disposal system. There are many sewers which have caved in or have been damaged due to blockage for years. The silt-level is so high in these sewers, that it would take 5 years or more to clear the blockages. Every year, water logged roads and traffic snarls during monsoons exposes the civic failure in cleaning the rot.

Protection from Excessive Noise

The problems of excessive noise in our residential areas are of increasing public health significance. What constitutes excessive noise? Noise apart from causing annoyance can cause damage to the auditory system. Prolonged exposure to sounds of 110 decibels is known to cause hearing damage. A healthful residential environment is one in which the background noise level is kept below 40-50 decibels, as per WHO report.

External noise control is often a function of urban planning, as many industrial processes and means of transportation are noisy by their very nature. Urban planning principles are meant to restrict noisy operations from residential areas. Noise pollution is the greatest ignored urban problem in Delhi. If Delhiites are to live peacefully in a close-packed urban setting, they must be able to count on limits to the noise the metropolis generates. We need to outlaw unnecessary, excessive, offensive, or unreasonable noise. However, we have to measure noise before we can regulate it. Some noise in Delhi is from loudspeakers blasting at social and religious functions. The city must design its regulations so as to control such noise.

Traffic noise ranges from 80 to 90 decibels. Music played on amplifiers is 120 decibels. Health experts say two years of regular exposure to 90 decibels will produce hearing loss. Excess noise is also a form of pollution, not an inevitable part of urban life. Environmentality have succeeded in cleaning the city's air and water to a large extent–but they have one more frontier to conquer—making Delhi quieter.

Urban Air Pollution

Besides being bad for individuals, pollution is bad for the economy. Once the true costs of air pollution are recognised, the case for action becomes clear. In Delhi, noisy activism by an organisation–the Centre for Science and Environment led to the Supreme Court Ruling that forced recalcitrant government officials to scrap dirty old diesel buses in favour of cleaner one that run on CNG.

Much has changed in the way we think about our environment. Our definition of the environment has broadened, our understanding of increasing threats has sharpened, but our ideas of how to protect and preserve our environment leaves much to be desired. Much of the dilemma springs from the explosion of population and resulting demands for transportation and energy (fossil fuel).

Global warming is the result of increasing atmosphere concentration of heat-trapping green house gases (GHG). The primary source of GHG is fossil fuel combustion oil (petrol) natural gas and coal–we need to reduce GHG emissions. As per KYOTO PROTOCOL-1997, international agreement to combat climate change, by cutting down GHG emissions by 5.2 per cent, below 1990 levels, by the period 2008-12.

The Government of the National Capital Territory of Delhi must push to meet clean air standards in Delhi. Spend on planting more trees and improve walkways and parks and our residential neighbourhoods. The State Government must introduce a policy to ensure that all the departments give weightage to environmental impacts in their decision making.

The idea is not just providing healthy air or conserving energy, but is also about increasing Delhi's competitive edge as a place where businesses, tourists seek-out.

Conservation of energy and renewable energy such as solar, wind and geothermal, lead not only to better air quality, but better public health.

Non-government organisations must help localities in the capital to get moving on sustainable energy issues. They must identify persons in Delhi who are already active on energy issues and bring them together to form a sort of coalition.

As a nation, still over whelmingly dependent on fossil fuel and foreign sources for its energy; now a land of petrol-guzzling vehicles in its cities, where the suburban spread model of urban development is perhaps just starting to be challenged.

Renewable energy, to become commercially viable may have a long way to go. But, nevertheless, it brooks no delay to make it happen in the interest of a sustainable, healthier environment in Delhi.

There are numerous small scale industries within residential areas of Old Delhi in particular, which are a health hazard to the residents. As per landuse policy these industries are non-confirming uses and need to be relocated. The Master Plan for Delhi 2021 offers no solution to relocation of these hazardous industries, to the detriment of residential environment.

Some of the other environmental hazards are the auto-repair workshops that encroach on road right-of-ways that inhibit safe pedestrian movement. The MPD-2021 has not addressed this problem, especially when the number of cars in Delhi keep increasing with corresponding demand for repairs.

Power Outages

In brutally hot summer of Delhi, when temperatures sore to 100° F or more, there are frequent power outages : Rajdhani Power Co. must explain to the people of Delhi why these outages occur–the reason behind them. The consequences of an interrupted power supply is devastating. Residential customers, should be compensated by the Power Company, who experience power outages. Business and industrial customers who qualify should also be compensated. Equipment failures, overloading, excessive heat or service outages caused by Rajdhani Power Co. employees, outages of 8 hours long or more, and customers who experience 3 outages of four hours long or more in a rolling 60-days period should also be eligible.

Outages caused by severe weather should not be covered for compensation. Amount of compensation to be determined by Rajdhani Power Co.–it should roughly equal to average residential bill and to be automatically mailed within 30 days to residential customers.

Customers can file claims for property lost or spoiled by outages, such as food that spoils if a refrigerator is off for several hours. Outages can mean lost business of thousands of rupees for the shop and business houses and industry. They are hit the hardest by frequent power outages. Hold Rajdhani Power Company accountable for power outages. Lack of power leaves most of Delhi in darkness much of the time, but people have learned to adjust somehow.

The problem of power, in addition to availability of power are in the delivery system. We lose about 40 per cent of electricity in transmission, that is sent over wires, its just wasted. We must develop transmission wires that conduct with no loss, which looks to be doable, with super conductivity system, then we'd have 40 per cent more electric power available. However, ultimate goal must be to prevent outages by increasing power generation capacity. These are many of the vexations of our current way of life.

Crime and the City

After over a decade of free market reforms, both poverty and economic inequality have risen. Privatization largely spawned a new generation of billionaires (crorepaties), while earnings for most of the population of the capital remains static if not worsened. A symptom of this malady is the spiraling crime rate, as the poor seem to take matters into their own hands. Gates manned by security guards are the symbol of crime ridden national capital.

Delhi was a safest city in India, but during the 1980s the face of crime changed in the national capital. Rapes, murders and burglaries are on the increase. Law enforcement breaking down.

One of the leading, if not paramount issue concerning the law and order administration in the capital, is the way we police the city, in the face of insurgent terrorism, crime (murders, rapes, burglary etc.) and other issues which have consequences, which the police must deal with, but over which the Delhi Police have little control. A safe environment and the perception of a safe environment are important to the long-term health of the capital.

A new vision of policing, one that joined the community and police in a mutually supportive partnership is required. It is necessary to go beyond merely arresting criminals; it is necessary to actually prevent crime in our neighbourhoods. Community policing is essential to ensure both the perception and reality of the public safety and quality of life in Delhi. It's bringing back the police on the beat, but in a modern way.

Community policing is, bringing police and residents into working partnerships, and giving the police responsibility for identifying and solving neighbourhood problems. Community policing works when it gives law-abiding residents the confidence needed to set clear standards and participate as partners with police in protecting their neighbourhoods.

Community policing is a working partnership between the police and the law-abiding public to prevent crime, arrest offenders, find solution to repeated problems and ultimately to enhance the quality of life in our city's neighbourhood. Community policing is to have a police constable, or police officer and their supervisors responsible for every street in the residential areas. These police officers must know the community well. They must form partnerships with community leaders not politicians to find solutions to recurring crime-related problems.

The goal of community policing is to transform big-city policing into a community-oriented game of police and residents. The police on the beat must listen to residents, work with resident leaders and groups. Welfare Associations must coordinate problem-solving activities with other government agencies, and use their authority and resources in ways that the public understands and approves.

(A) Delhi's–Man-made Environment

City is a man-made environment. It represents great human achievement. Human ingenuity and skills that built several Delhi's reflect the culture of a particular period. Prince Charles of England in his book 'Vision of Britain' writes that: "The design of the built-environment as it affects people and the lives they live, should concern us".

The built-environment of Delhi metropolis is reflected in its various types of buildings, their volume, scale, texture and colour; in its urban spaces such as plazas, parks and roads; in its street furniture like signage, advertisements, street lighting; and in its mobile elements like the vehicular traffic.

This man-made environment as we see today, is a physical expression of the social, economic and technological conditions of the age we live in. It mirrors society at this given period of time. Delhi's buildings can be no greater than the sense of responsibility and patronage from which they originate. Most of the structures all over Delhi violate building standards in someway, hastily thrown up by the builders with the connivance of the city officials and politicians, without regard to construction code or building bye-laws.

In many arenas of this great metropolis, politics, private interest, commercial greed, urban planning and architectural design clash. Results show up clearly in the profiles, skylines and silhouettes of the national capital. They show up in its many genres of city planning and urban design, ranging from the grandiose to the organic and humble.

The old cities of India, whether resulting from planning or organic growth, reflected multiple level of organisations. There was an identifiable hierarchy of intricately linked functions, spaces and movement systems, from the scale of the city as a whole, through that of the front door of the house. In the walled city of Delhi built by Shahjehan, the main streets from city gates to its centre defined identifiable quarters, directing the placement of public spaces, buildings, bazaars and other elements of the townscape. The walled city at the time had a character and a local identity which lent to its imagability. Today, we see walled city as urban jungle, where the profiteers and the motor vehicles rule.

The urban form of the walled city of Delhi worked itself out, subject only to the respect for custom, ownership, and the Muslim's right to individual privacy. The concern for privacy determined, where doors and windows would be placed on building fronts, and how high buildings would rise. More basically, this concern asserted itself in the introversion of the house, the appearance towards the street being unimportant. At the same time, the traditional grouping of attached courtyard houses expressed a degree of interdependence among neighbouring structures.

In Old Delhi (walled city) the primary street carry the bazaars, with the large retail and wholesale outlets. Production, storage and service centres are immediately behind, set in the clearly defined residential neighbourhoods or mohallas. Secondary streets run as spines of commercial and residential activity through the mohallas. At the junction of two or more streets, chowks provide some breathing room in the high density of the city.

The outcome of this rational organisation, is not a formal layout, since it did not start as one, neither was there any prescriptive guidance, to steer it into a geometrically unadulterated outline. The structure of the urban form possess, the sort of coherence, demonstrated by the walled city of Delhi, and this is in the absence of municipal authority, to police and articulate public space, only because the social structure was well formulated, and tradition stood as the guarantor of a consistent modus operandi. Without the force of tradition and a consolidated social agenda, unsupervised city-making will succumb to disorder.

Old Delhi, the walled city of Delhi known as Shahjahanabad, was once the pride of the Mughals and amongst the world's most beautiful medieval cities. That glorious city today is history. Population pressure, commercialization, unauthorised constructions, and blatant neglect by Municipal Corporation of Delhi, has reduced the walled city to its present state of congestion and chaos.

The deterioration of the walled city began with the Partition of India in 1947, which brought in waves of refugees from Pakistan. The refugees started their small shops on the pavements of Chandni Chowk, Khari Bawli and Dariba Kalan. Today, Old Delhi is the hub of commercial activities, and presents a dismal picture of congestion, chaotic traffic and sub-human living conditions. It's virtually one big slum.

After independence there was a great building boom leading to changes to Delhi's urban environment. The cruel irony of Delhi's building boom is that, while it breaths vitality into the central business district of Connaught

Place, at the same time it drains beauty from the skyline. These emerging buildings are almost totally bereft of any character.

Architecture is supposed to be an art with which we live, visual blight leaves everybody a little poorer, at least in spirit. This underscores two key issues–how to reconcile massive new projects with intimately scaled old buildings and how to shape new high-rise buildings that etch a distinctive skyline silhouette. A high-rise building has to work on two visual scales–one smaller addressed to the passerby on the street, the other much larger, directed to the grand sweep of the skyline. There is no substitute to creativity if Delhi's building activity is going to leave an artistic legacy and not just skyscraper, size or profit to satisfy commercial greed. The presence of characterless buildings on the skyline makes it a visual bore.

Truly our designers and builders have foregone the opportunity to make a statement on Delhi's skyline. It appears Delhi's post-independence architecture has not brought enough creativity to the drafting board. Town planning, until 1930 considered a humanistic discipline based upon history, aesthetics, and culture has became a technical profession based upon numbers–'Statistics'. The planners no longer employ the vocabulary of civic art, nor do they find the opportunity to practice it. Planners are today chiefly preoccupied with administrative procedure such as development controls, files, in short bureaucracy.

We have lost the art of how to build things well. Lost the art of architecture and urban design. The builders do not have the ability to discern the good from the bad. Delhi's roads run through an urban landscape that is littered with ugly buildings and commercial messages.

We have been rebuilding Delhi for cars rather than for people. In recent decades, car-oriented, anticity projects have intruded upon, if not destroyed, sections of Delhi, wiping out streets and urbanism in their wake. The ever increasing use of cars is altering the face of the nation's capital, in the process the special values of Delhi are being sacrificed to the function of the automobile.

Motorised transportation is undoubtedly critical for Delhi metropolis. But it is too important, to be seen only as a means of moving people, goods and services, rather it has to be seen as a means of designing a more satisfying urban environment. Because much that would be done to improve the environment, would also help improve transportation. It is, therefore, essential to develop principles and techniques to link effectively the handling of transportation with the designing or restructuring Delhi.

Delhi's aesthetic qualities, its livability, and its quality of life are far more than merely a luxury and taste, they are important factors in retaining existing business and attracting new ones. Scenic vistas, scenic roads, and similar intangible aesthetic features contribute immeasurably to the city's image and sense of place. Realising the fragility of these aesthetic resources, it is necessary to create comprehensive programmes to protect and enhance these assets. We need to enact laws to enhance the quality of life by preserving the character and the desirable aesthetic features of Delhi.

What Mughals built in mid-Seventeenth Century and the British in early Twentieth Century, without the aristocracy to patronise, the monumental architecture disappeared after independence. Cheap, non-descript architecture and fragmentation of communities fostered by an increasingly mobile car-oriented culture. Poor urban planning has led to the decline of the national capital.

The post-independence urban form that has emerged in Delhi is reflected in the massive Central Government employees housing colonies, developed by the Central Public Works Department, the Delhi Development Authority's housing for various income groups, the Cooperative Housing Society's housing on plotted and group-housing development, and finally the private housing by private developers and builders. The DDA has built dreary public housing. It's characterless group housing, facades musty with mildew have cropped up like weeds all over metropolitan Delhi. Built with cheap materials in a vulgar style has made Delhi ugly. In certain parts, however, there are some beautiful buildings.

The predominant land use being residential, the built-form in residential areas of Delhi assumes significance and reflects to a great extent the image of the nation's capital. Housing form is greatly influenced by its relation to settlement forms. External constraints of overall layout affects internal design of the house.

The urban community consists of wide variety of social groups–The rural lifestyle of migrant squatters and the westernised urban life style of rich, all coexist side by side reflecting contrasting built-form pattern, ranging from the palatial bungalow to the multi-storeyed flats, the inner city "Katra" and the mud-walled jhuggi. This duality is becoming more pronounced with about 30 per cent of Delhi's urban population living in slums and squatter settlements.

Housing development in the capital is regulated by development controls–like land subdivision regulations, building bye-laws and zoning, designed to promote health, safety, morals and welfare of the residents. A large portions of housing is built outside the framework of the regulations. The building bye-laws specify structural standards, internal dimensions of rooms, light and ventilation, setbacks, coverages on plots. Bye-laws ensure safety of residents, proper light and ventilation. Densities and floor spaces are specified keeping in view the capacity of infrastructure. Height of buildings is regulated in order to provide adequate day light, fire-fighting requirements. Delhi's bye-laws are normative and prescriptive resulting in monotonous regimental residential patterns.

The built-environment of post-independence Delhi and its suburbs, as we perceive it, can be characterised as an amorphous mass of sordidness, punctuated with patches of pompous and vulgar hideousness, in the garb of so-called "modern architecture". Visually as well as functionally, much of man-made townscape of Delhi metropolis, appears so chaotic, as to defy any comprehension, as most of it contains such incessant repetition, to the extent of being monotonous to the eye of the beholder. The fact that so much of the built-form in Delhi is unimaginative and of poor quality, is a reflection of a generally poor level of understanding and appreciation in our urban society, of the importance of architecture and urban design in the city building process.

Over the years Delhi has been expanding haphazardly. In fact this phenomenon of its growing into amorphous mass of structures has been the dominant feature of urban expansion. This built-form of the metropolis as we see today is engendered by the initiative and enterprise of developers and builders acting individually and collectively. This community action, therefore, needs to be guided, through urban design, expressing the basic principles and design guidelines, which should help shape the urban form of Delhi. Architects and urban designers must design, with sensitivity and imagination, so that people in Delhi can live in more pleasant surroundings.

One of the main objectives of the very first Delhi Plan, 1981, was to combine utilitarian solutions to urban development problems, with the maximum of urban design for aesthetic effects. The planners recognised that a great capital of India deserves great architecture or the maximum of which a generation is capable, and this it had not been getting, in its individual buildings, in its housing development, nor has there been attention to the civic ensemble, the square, the vista. Opportunities were being tragically ignored. The Delhi Plan, 1962 placed special emphasis on this aspect, not just verbally, but by illustrations and prototypes, which was graphically presented in the publication entitled "Nineth Delhi".

Urban planning is not only a matter of allotting land for various needs of the city, it is also very much concerned with the form of development and indeed with the aesthetic quality of the environment that is eventually produced. Experience has shown, that the concept of "Zonal Development Plan" embodied in the Delhi Plan, 1981, which by implication is the basis of physical development, has proved grossly inadequate, because the issues relating to the urban form of the environment are ignored in such two-dimensional exercises. Besides, the "Zonal Development Plans" are practically of no use for areas of the city that are built-up or even partially built.

Biologists say, man's life is a struggle with his environment, therefore, man's struggle is with himself, for the city is an environment of his own making, unintentional and unforeseen as many of the results may be. Cities have no existence apart from the people who live and work in them. They have no dynamism apart from that given them by their populations. The city is disorderly because we are unmindful of disorder, or lacking in the means to achieve order. The city is ugly, because we either do not care about aesthetics and beauty or we are not able to produce it. The city is sinking into decay, because we have lost the wish or the vigour to maintain it.

The city of Paris for instance is praiseworthy, because of its civic arts, for the excellence of its man-made artifacts and the superb inter-relation of the buildings and public realm. One of the keys to Paris's beauty lies in the rigorous regulations instituted by Georges Eugene Haussmann, who redesigned the city in the mid-Nineteenth Century dealing with everything from building heights to roof configurations, which lent the city a sense of order, unity and coherence.

Delhi's urban life can be wonderfully rewarding, and certainly possesses the means to make it so. That kind of civic self-consciousness, is exactly what is missing in Delhi.

In the early 1970s the Government of India being seised of the imminent danger to the aesthetic character of the national capital, introduced legislative measures to regulate and even control the quality of the built-form by enacting the Delhi Urban Art Commission Act, 1973 and establishing the Delhi Urban Art Commission in 1974.

The extent to which the aesthetic quality of Delhi's urban environment would be preserved and developed, rested upon the vitality of DUAC and the measure of its influence on the Central Government, as well as the local authorities in the Capital. Maintaining its own image was as important as improving the image of the national capital.

Unfortunately, the style of functioning of the DUAC leaves much to be desired. There is a popular feeling that the Commission is a 'fifth wheel' in the chariot of sanctioning authorities. The DUAC has reduced its role to mere scrutiny of building projects placed before it, overlooking the major issues of environmental design of the city. The DUAC Act, 1973, clearly states that the Commission is to advise the Central Government in the matter of preserving, developing and maintaining the aesthetic quality of urban and environmental design of Delhi, and to advise and guide local authorities in respect of any project of building and engineering operation or any development proposal, which affects or is likely to affect the aesthetic quality of the surroundings or any public amenity provided therein.

To what extent has the DUAC lived up to the letter and spirit of the Act? It's existence for past 30 years has not created any impact on the aesthetic quality of the built-form in the metropolis of Delhi. It's time for the DUAC to dust off its copy of the DUAC Act. If there are shortcomings, the Commission should not be afraid to have them pointed out and criticised, because the Commission is meant to protect and enhance the aesthetic quality of Delhi. Now that it has been pointed out the DUAC should move to correct things. In recent years, the DUAC has found less and less meaningful work to do. The DUAC's raioson d'être has largely evaporated.

The most important reason for its failure is that in the absence of an overall urban design in a conceptual form, at least, for the key areas of the capital, the method of judging architectural or development projects placed before the DUAC tend to be subjective and arbitrary in the sanctioning process. Architecture to be of value and valued, cannot be conceived without the consciousness of the environment it creates. Architecture cannot be taken out of its environmental context.

The problem faced in Delhi is that the architect, even if he does all he can to relate the building he has designed to its surroundings, has actually no control over what happens off the plot of land he has been commissioned to consider. The DDA on the other hand tends to regard a particular land use merely as an allocation of resource to be parceled out for zoning purposes, without much understanding of its three-dimensional characteristics or the nature of the building that will be placed on it. Such an approach to urban development has produced stereotyped and unimaginative buildings. A city is not just an assembly of buildings, it is a community for enrichment of life. Its attractiveness depends on the design and layout of buildings and the relationship between open spaces and built-up areas. What is actually needed is the design of the city and not just the buildings per se.

In fact the DUAC in its very first Annual Report, 1974–75, stated that "in the absence of a well defined objective and a conceptualised urban design framework for Delhi, it would be difficult for the Commission to render effective advice to the Government in the matter of preserving and developing the aesthetic quality and environmental design in Delhi". The DUAC had expressed the urgency of preparing an overall Concept Plan, and a comprehensive approach to study the aesthetic features and characteristics of the national capital.

The study of the aesthetic characteristics of urban Delhi are largely made apparent through visual perception of the surroundings, so that we understand the underlying aesthetic relationship among the visually significant three-dimensional forms of which Delhi is composed. It is only then there will be a satisfactory basis for understanding Delhi, in terms of the aesthetic quality of its urban environment, and consequently of identifying areas whose aesthetic character needs, either to be preserved, improved or further developed.

The Delhiites must know that the DUAC and the DDA are the authorities whose responsibility it is to address this vital aspect of urban development.

Urban Aesthetics

As stated earlier, urban planning is not simply a matter of allotting land for various kinds of development. It should be equally concerned with the form of development and the quality of the physical environment. Ultimately what matters is not simply where development occurs, its form and quality are equally important, as our planning process will always be judged in the final analysis by the quality of results it produces.

In fact the origin of city-planning and its early development possessed a strong aesthetic orientation, and that issues of urban aesthetics have long been closely linked with the basic objectives of urban planning. Urban aesthetics must be accorded a far more important role now in a comprehensive approach to urban development.

Kevin Lynch in his book "The Form of Cities", writes about urban areas possessing distinct and recordable qualities that affect peoples' perceptual satisfaction with the urban environment. Several considerations determine urban form, structure and quality : the placement of key functional areas and buildings, the location of circulation routes, the siting of residential and other areas with regard to key reference points, orientation, prevailing winds, existing vistas, and so on. A systematic study of these elements and their relationship to each other should be an essential component of the city planning process. Without it, creativity will be absent.

Prof. Sidney Williams in his book on 'Urban Aesthetic', has suggested an approach to the study of the aesthetic characteristics of cities. The visual survey technique outlined by Williams consists of two parts. The first identifies the three-dimensional characteristics of the city, i.e., site and the man-made features which have been added to it. The second records significant paths and vantage points from which the city can be perceived. For the first part of the visual survey the city-site is classified into six forms:

1. Level, gently sloping or rolling sites;
2. Sloping sites backed by hills or steeper slopes;
3. Valley or gorge sites;
4. Amphi-theatrical or fan shaped sites;
5. Bowl-shaped sites; and
6. Ridge or hill-top sites;

The man-made features are classified into five forms:

1. Urban texture;
2. Green areas;

3. Circulation facilities;
4. Paved open spaces; and
5. Individually significant architectural masses, including vertical and horizontal forms.

For the second part of the visual survey, Williams has developed five ways through which the city may be perceived and experienced : the panorama, the skyline, the vista, urban open space, and through the experience of the individual motion.

It was Hassan Fathy, an Egyptian Architect, who said: "That every generation that has produced architecture, has evolved its own favourite forms, as peculiar to that generation, as its language, or its folk lore". He further goes on to say : "Until the collapse of cultural frontiers, during the Twentieth Century, there were distinctively local shapes and details in architecture, and the buildings in any locality were beautiful. Today, we have buildings transplanted to an alien environment". In the past socio-cultural and climatic factors were strong determinants of built-form; today market forces are shaping the built-form of Delhi.

In today's Delhi for instance, there is no indigenous style. The houses of the rich and poor alike are without character. The tradition is lost, and we have been cut off from the past. The obsession with so called modernity, which accompanied the early years of independence, was a major characteristic of the new development and architecture.

Frank Lloyed Wright, greatest architect of our times, believed that architecture was civilization's chief form of expression. In the great Gothic Cathedrals of the Twelfth and Thirteenth Centuries, for example, all the energy of the arts–sculpture, painting, music–was poured into the building. But with the invention of the printing press, and the widespread dispersal of books, everything changed. Ideas became portable. They no longer had to be expressed in an edifice. "Architecture", as Wright observed, "is dethroned". The question is how can architecture reassert itself?

Man's innate need for beauty, the why and wherefore of the pleasure and satisfaction, experienced through stimulus and response generated by the sight or touch of certain forms, the emotions stirred within us by colours and rhythmic lines, that even in concrete objects seems to flow while they stand stolidly rooted to the ground. Beauty in objects around us, provide visual comfort. Good taste and greater opportunity to live in intimacy, with beauty, should not be the privilege of the few, but the common inheritance of all. To bring elegance and grace into an otherwise harsh and drab human existence. People yearn for something beyond the satisfaction of mere creature comforts and needs.

Street Picture

Delhiites must understand how much their environment affects their quality of life, and how they can best serve their own needs by improving the physical surroundings. In a diverse metropolis of Delhi, where social, cultural and spiritual realities vary, the physical environment is the one thing 'that Delhiites truly share, which makes it all the more important to work on it together.

I am sure you would enjoy having a pleasant view of your city while driving in a car, bus or a commuter train, or walking, and would not like looking at junk, ugly buildings, clutter of sign boards and hoardings, unsightly electric and telephone poles, or garbage littered. You would definitely prefer travelling or walking along well landscaped streets of Delhi. The metropolis of Delhi should be made exciting to look at.

A road in Delhi is not only a means of communication from one place to another, but it must also offer some dignity of approach to important buildings and be a pleasant way for the passerby. Like the Rajpath which offers some dignity of approach to the capital complex on Raisina Hill. It is a visual and spatial experience of a place through moving along Rajpath. One does get a better perception of Delhi, while moving along its roads. The city government should consider sharpening the distinction between one road and another, so that each travel corridor evolves its own identity. As an aspect of urban design, the city/metropolis can infuse character into its transportation corridors by formulating a vision of what each road should look like. The city government should draw up guidelines that reinforce the most prominent traits of several major road corridors like the Ring Roads, the arterial roads.

Unfortunately, the conscious aesthetic discernment, the ability to recognize the ugly and the beautiful, per se, is not a common quality. People have become so used to living among surroundings in which beauty has little or no place. There is a decline in the relevance and influence of the architectural profession in India–(Delhi). Trained to be among the most wide-ranging problem-solvers in the world, architects need to rededicate themselves to their city. Those few architects who have made consistent efforts to engage the public will insist that it is indeed a rewarding endeavour. Architects who can design with sensitivity and imagination, so that people of Delhi can live in more pleasant surroundings. It is unfortunate, that our 'welfare state' ideology has contributed very little to urban planning and design, as an idea or a programme. Quality of life should become a national concern. Only then will design become increasingly useful as both a decision-making tool and a generator of value. The city beautiful movement was a period of urban rebuilding and new-town construction in which civic pride, beauty and community were a consensus agenda.

The developments and builders must be aware that development controls and building bye-laws, inevitably shape buildings they construct, and that these designs consequences can or should be anticipated; subdivision of land into plots and roads for residential development, is not just a way of providing plots for sale, but that it shapes new residential neighbourhood; building public housing by CPWD, DDA or MCD is not just a way of providing shelter, but creation of communities; urban redevelopment is not just the removal of slums and blighted buildings, but a strategy for reorganising the new areas.

We need to rewrite development regulations (Building Bye-laws) to ensure that appropriate design relationships are achieved. There are some successful examples of urban design, such as the creation of Paris. Paris has been imposing design guidelines for more than two centuries. From 1784 onwards, Parisian legislation related building height to street widths and imposed a setback angle for attics. Façade controls were imposed for important streets. This one simple idea which affected the design of city of Paris, encouraged architects/designers to return to the elements of city design that were pushed aside by the doctrine of modernism but that turned out to be necessary for a coherent city. However, these concepts were expressed as relatively abstract, formal guidelines as stylistically neutral as possible.

We must regain by conscious effort, the essential unity of function and form. It is not a question of inventing a 'City beautiful'. It is a question of discovering the form that will most clearly give expression to the function of our city—the national capital, as the form of the old city reflected its way of living.

We are making Delhiites accustomed to urban ugliness, in place of an orderly and beautiful city. In order to promote urban design, it is essential to organise a 'National City Beautiful Exposition', where India's well known architects, urban-designers, landscape architects and city planners, working in coalition, provide a glimpse of an urban environment built more carefully, than the existing ones. Many visitors to such an EXPO, accustomed to urban ugliness in their cities, will see for the first time a splendid example of urban design, and make them wonder why their cities could not be as orderly and beautiful as portrayed in the EXPO.

The work of these experts, in their respective professions, must show that they are the guardians of social and aesthetic life, maintaining and enhancing the traditional values of the community for the future generations.

If the citizens of Delhi really wanted to build great place in which to live and work, they would have to do more to make them happen. They would have to build more than the isolated monumental structures of the city beautiful. They would require a broader understanding of the desire to shape the patterns that define the character of a place, its streets and streetscapes. Civic reforms should become a national grass-root movement.

Urban Trees

Trees offer substantial benefits to cities. They provide cityscape ornamentation and very often much-needed architectural mitigation. Architect Frank Lloyed Wright had a famous saying : "When a doctor makes a mistake he buries it; when an architect makes a mistake he plants a tree".

By shading sidewalks, streets and parks, trees provide physiological comfort and their presence exerts a beneficial psychological effect on people. Trees also shade buildings, thereby decreasing air-conditioning and conserve energy. Due to their dense foliage, trees are a natural screens to dissipate noise, block wind, dust and provide privacy. Trees have a crucial impact on the natural environment by absorbing moisture and carbon dioxide and emitting oxygen. Trees contribute to soil and water conservation by slowing the amount of water runoff and reducing soil erosion.

Landscape design should be carefully considered at the planning stage of buildings. Often regarded as merely a cosmetic afterthought, landscape design can make a significant contribution to improving the environmental impact of a building or urban area.

Urban designers must recognise that the small green leaf is one of natures' most amazing technicians as a preserver of the environment. Leaves breathe in carbon dioxide and other gases released by motor vehicles and industry, and turn them back to the atmosphere as oxygen. Their hairy surfaces catch particles and keep soot from saturating the air. They also smother noise—traffic noise by as much as 60 per cent. Their bare tracery or their lovely green shapes enrich the landscape. Writing about the Friendly Trees, Henry Van Dyke states: "He that planteth a tree is the servant of God. He provideth a kindness for many generations, and faces that he hath not seen shall bless him.

I think that I shall never see a poem lovely as a tree– says Joyce Kilmer.

Protection of Historic Landmark Buildings

How much of historic Delhi, how much of our national heritage will be left for generations yet to be born? And what does it say about us in Delhi, of our values, of our regard for those who will follow. Can we, as citizens stand by while others destroy historic Delhi, in the name of so-called corporate profits.

Conservation of historic places cannot be justified by economics alone. This built environment is our collective memory, it is not just the work of an individual builder, rather it is the work of a civilization. We destroy or abuse the past, we destroy all we have inherited. On the other hand saving our heritage of older buildings and neighbourhoods, does not mean we want to live in the past, on the contrary it encourages each generation to build in its own style, to meet its own needs. However, it also recognises that we cannot afford to reject history, the culture, the traditions and values on which our lives and futures are built. We must identify architecture that celebrates Delhi's history and personality—a sense of place.

We do not have the wherewithall to save every building or place, nor should we try. We must apply the concept of sustainable development, which translates into growth that meets the economic needs of living generation, without spoiling assets for generations that follow. Every place must identify its strongest and most distinctive features and develop them or run the risk of being all things to all persons and nothing special to any. Nobelauret Robert Solow, put it this way : "Livability is not some middle-class luxury. It is an economic imperative".

Historic Districts

Buildings, structures, and associated objects and land that possess a recognised historic or architectural value. The Delhi Urban Arts Commission should be empowered to restrict or control changes to exterior architectural features visible from public ways. Such areas/districts should be eligible for Central Government funds to facilitate conservation. Chicago's internationally famed Michigan Avenue. "Streetwall" facing Grant Park has been given local landmark recognition and protection. Property tax incentive to apply to both landmark residential structures and to "contributing" structures within landmark districts. This nationally innovative programme already had helped encourage the owners of more than a dozen deteriorating commercial landmarks to rehabilitate them, thus bringing them back on the tax rolls. Structures are listed as "significant" in the city's historic survey. Financial incentives are provided to help owners of historic properties find ways to reuse their great architectural assets. Conservation and renewal of historic buildings, districts (areas), and landscape affirm the continuity and evolution of urban society.

The walled-city of Delhi, that once produced uniquely acculturated architectural forms has been invaded by a tide of buildings in post-independence era, unrelated to indigenous traditions. A medieval city largely composed of vernacular structures, some abandoned, others decayed and forgotten. The mohallas of Old Delhi were the neighbourhoods of everyday life, a testimony of human capacity to endow the built environment with grace and meaning.

Much of the national capital's remarkable colonial heritage is consumed in the process of rebuilding. The obliteration of cross-cultural Indian and European tropical architectural form is resented by our conservationists but very little done to prevent the destruction of historic urban environment. We need an aggressive conservation programme to protect the character of our urban heritage.

The national capital–Delhi must become the source of positive vision of its inhabitants, in which all have a safe, healthy and sustainable urban environment. We need new vision, long-term perspective and above all bold leadership to succeed.

(B) The Way We Live

Three distinct urban patterns characterise the cityscape of the national capital—Delhi: We have the high-density Old City of Delhi—Designed by Emperor Shahjahan in mid-Seventeenth Century, with its traditional mohallas, havellis; followed by the low density New City of Delhi, designed by Sir Edwin Lutyen in early Twentieth Century, with its colonial-era bungalows; and the post-independence medium to high density spontaneous city–a generated suburban development, as against imposed. The resultant pattern is irregular or organic. This irregular part of the city is the result of development left entirely to private developers and cooperative societies. Had the development authority subdivided land in an orderly manner and disposed of it, before it is handed over to the users, a uniformly patterned city would have emerged. Some of the good examples of residential areas developed by CPWD are Jor Bagh, Golf Links, and Sunder Nagar.

During the course of last fifty years, a large number of residential areas have been developed by the Central Public Works Department, private developers, cooperative housing societies and the Delhi Development Authority, within Delhi and its suburbs. Most of these residential areas, irrespective of the income levels of their inhabitants, seem visually monotonous and characterless. Functionally, and aesthetically a failure. In many of these areas the pressures of rapid urban growth have eroded the neighbourliness, peace and quiet that drew the inhabitants to set roots there in the first place. The residential areas are laid out strictly for the convenience of developers, with hardly a thought to civic art.

Sadly, Delhi's residential areas are a mere geometrical arrangement of streets and houses, and irrespective of the income groups they house, are cold and monotonous and characterless, with built-in traffic hazards that imperil pedestrian safety. Post-independence suburbs in Delhi are different from their predecessors. They are mere subdivisions of land into plots and streets, with very little artistry in the way they are planned. Scale also differentiates the post-independence suburban development—they are huge !

A residential neighbourhood is much more than a geometrical arrangement of streets, plots and houses, which our residential areas are ! The house, that an architect designs on the residential plot, is the basis of the home for the family. But a larger community needs a physical environment—indeed a neighbourhood in which there is space, opportunity for activities and a well organised and efficient social life, in which residents seek each other's company and contribute to the proper utilisation of time, in order to produce higher values of national and social culture.

The residential area should be planned as a physical and social entity, a more or less self-sufficient community with a definite boundary and certain required components. Proximity and convenience are primary factors, in most of the activities on which neighbourhood planning should be based, like everyday household shopping, children's education, recreation and health service, access to city bus and rapid transit or main urban highway. Every facility used by the people has some sort of "catchment" area—geographical area served by day-to-day requirements of the residents. Normally a ten-minute walk is approximately half a mile distance from the edge, to the centre of the residential neighbourhood,—conceptualised as the determinant of neighbourhood size.

Neighbourhoods should be laid out so that in a few minutes, residents can walk from their homes to parks, stores, services, and other amenities of daily life. By organising the neighbourhood on a pedestrian scale and making room for neighbourhood stores, services and recreation areas, local gathering places will have a better chance of coming into being. Today, walking within our residential areas is an exercise in courage. Motor vehicles zoom along the streets, sidewalks are non-existent; bicycling is difficult because the sidewalks where they exist are too narrow and streets too full of speeding motor vehicles. We need pedestrian-friendly neighbourhoods in Delhi, with wide enough sidewalks, so that people can walk without fear of getting clogged by a car.

Neighbourhood streets must be designed with children's and pedestrian safety in mind. They include sharp curves and other traffic engineering techniques designed to limit vehicles to low speed and to prevent through traffic, which is so common in our residential areas. The pressures of urbanisation are eroding the neighbourliness and peace and quiet. We have to restore the peace and tranquility, which has been lost in Delhi's sprawling suburban landscape. We need residential neighbourhood, where errands can be made by walking instead of driving as we do now, where you know the neighbours up and down the street. All of us have that simple longing to mute the stresses, noises and irritations of our hectic city life.

Through the centuries, societies have spawned informal gathering places where the stresses of work and home can be left behind for a while. The companionship of others is important, it is instinctive to human nature. Our residential areas lack places where residents can go in hopes of striking up conversation with others. Sorry to say, that clubs in some residential areas are more akin to restaurants for weekend entertainment and celebrations. As there are no informal gathering places, many opportunities for making friendships and pursuing common interests have disappeared.

How have the suburbs exacerbated the stress of daily life and what better alternatives can be found. People need a 'third place' outside of work and home, where they can make contact with others. The companionship of others is an important balm. It is instinctive to human nature, we deny it at our peril.

Our residential areas lack a physical core that helps establish their identity. The homes, shops and other public buildings do not have architectural elements in common, that make these structures look like they belong together. Instead the residential areas resemble countless 'faceless' residential areas all over Delhi. Streetscapes in each part of the residential neighbourhood, should be punctuated by focal points–parks, community centre, shopping, public buildings, that lend identity to each neighbourhood. The principle is, that the foremost issue in designing a layout of a neighbourhood should be concern for the people rather than their motor vehicles.

Delhi's sprawling post-independence suburbs have no heart, no central core, no sense of place that residents can lean on, take pride in or turn to in times of celebration. After doing without it for fifty years Delhiites must recognise and articulate their hunger for a public realm. We must together call for the return of a sense of community. We must make the developers, planners, architects and Municipal Corporation of Delhi, Delhi Development Authority, Delhi Urban Art Commission, answer the call in practical and innovative ways.

Sanctioning authorities in Delhi must accept only those residential neighbourhood plans, which are designed with sensitivity and imagination, so that residents can live in more pleasing surroundings, other than the non-discript, mediocre buildings, found everywhere. It is the lack of this kind of thinking that makes the residential areas in Delhi, so much like a hundred other residential developments. The ugliness of the houses in which people live does not unduly depress most of them. They get upset or depressed on the issue of amenities, like, water, electricity than on questions of proportion and relationships of architectural forms.

Residential neighbourhoods are more than places to live, they are interactive components of a larger urban system. The residential neighbourhood is a fundamental unit of civic culture. Neighbourhood organisations, like Residents' Welfare Associations in Delhi, should become an integral, ongoing and significant basis of civil life in the capital. It will be a community-led initiative to bring about healthier progressive Delhi. It will be like managing the city from the community base.

Open Spaces

Requirements for public open spaces in residential areas, have been reduced to a set of regulations that are primarily statistical. The requirements say little about the configuration and quality of open spaces. Usually, the main specification is a per centage of the site area. Since there is no stipulation about its design, developers, distribute the required acreage, from the residue left over after roads and plots are laid out, neglecting the fact that people use open spaces in specific ways. Precise standards must be established for the full range of traditional open spaces, so notably absent in our residential areas. Only specific standards will produce the specific open spaces that support specific activities. Without them, open spaces will only describe the dribble of green that is left over after the developer has finished laying out the plots and streets.

There is no civic life in our city. We are becoming an insular society. People seem to be withdrawing from public life into the shelter of their private homes. Many factors contribute to this condition. One of them is our changing physical environment, which has led to the perceived decline in civic life. Community cannot form in the absence of communal space, without places for people to get-together to talk and interact, socialize. Just as it is difficult to imagine the concept of family independent of the home, it is near-impossible to imagine community independence of the town square.

The vast metropolis of Delhi has become depersonalised, hence the restoration of neighbourly communities would tend to humanise it. The concept of neighbourhood, reflects a general reaction against the monotonous and wasteful pattern of urban development. It's not only Delhi, but all the cities in India, have accustomed society to the paradox of collective living, of separate and individualistic families. This has led to the habit of living together, without the sense of togetherness, of concentration of people, without emotional integration. Sociologists attribute three basic factors, to the creation of a community life in a residential neighbourhood. Community consciousness, togetherness, and emotional integration. These three factors together produce security and an atmosphere of creative and cooperative living in all pursuits of life. Such a philosophy must, therefore, dominate the design of a house and of the residential neighbourhood.

Residential Pattern

Delhi's residential pattern consists of the traditional inner city housing, the organic-urban villages, the unplanned squatter settlements, and unauthorised colonies; colonial bungalows of New Delhi area, planned plotted detached houses—private housing, DDA housing and Cooperative housing, Row Housing in resettlement colonies, DDA plotted housing and group housing–both cooperative and DDA.

Residential neighbourhoods and communities vary economically and socially. There is also difference between the older parts of the city, characterised by high population densities and congestion, as against newer residential areas which have been developed on planning principles and standards.

Planning standards are not prescribed on the basis of income groups–high, middle, low and weaker sections. For instance, the standards of services like water supply, sewerage and electricity in squatter settlements, slums and low income housing areas are much lower than those in middle and high income areas.

Shopping facilities also vary according to income groups. Hut shops, street vending, mobile shops on wheels, open platform markets are characteristics of shopping in middle and high income areas are relatively formal in corporating buildings and commodities of much higher quality and standard.

Across the Government of NCT of Delhi border, into Gurgaon District of Haryana State, thousands of hectares of farm land and open spaces, are filled with largely formless, soulless houses and buildings, unconnected to one another, except by the dependence on the car. Residents spend more time driving from one place to another and less time with one another.

The resulting urban form in this exurbia of Delhi Metropolis is too congested to be efficient, too chaotic to be beautiful, and too dispersed to possess the diversity and vitality of a great city. The multistoreyed residential buildings are built in highly urbanised area of Delhi and are supposed to be of a high-density, yet no effort is made to ensure the continuity of built-up and open spaces, which is an essential element for an attractive urban environment.

Revitalising Neighbourhoods

How can we improve the character of the neighbourhoods, which make up the suburbs in Delhi? We need to fill in and heighten the quality of the places already in existence in Delhi. We should seize the potential of making the suburbs more satisfying. The suburban development has created a pattern of residential enclaves without the other infrastructure of civic life–civic amenities.

Many Delhiites must feel, that the residential areas in which they live, whose form and character they did not choose, they were imposed upon them by the local developers and builders. Builders tried more than ever to maximise the coverage of their building plots. Houses are built of windowless inside rooms, strung from front to rear, depriving even their outer rooms of light and ventilation. The rear yard is reduced to dingy, lightless courts only good for hanging clothes.

The residents feel that there is something wrong with the houses they live in, their neighbourhoods, the city itself, the whole physical arrangements of their lives. They yearn to belong somewhere, to be members of real communities. But the feelings aren't moored to specific ideas about what it takes to make a good place. Delhiites should begin, by understanding how much their environment affects their quality of life. Once this is recognised, it becomes obvious how we can best serve our own needs by improving the physical surroundings.

As a people we are not in the habit of thinking critically about our environment, or about how its form can dramatically affect the quality of our lives. Even a higher standard of living has somehow failed to result in a better quality of life. The residential areas in Lutyen's New Delhi, have in some areas curved streets lined with trees. The trees were planted at formal intervals on all the residential streets. The formality of the trees connected the sprawled properties, at the same time they provide a sense of shelter on the street—streets that invited walking. Compare this to our residential neighbourhoods to-day, where streets have no other function except to funnel the cars to and fro. We need to redesign the streets for pedestrian safety for making our neighbourhoods more livable.

Neotraditional development—new interpretation of traditional communities that aim to conjure nostalgia for bygone architectural styles, for the safe and friendly atmosphere of small towns. Where, everybody can walk to school, to buy grocery around the corner, and to their house of worship. Individuals isolated from one another are powerless. Whereas individuals who form an active local society, gain the ability to influence conditions, people coming together, discussing their concerns, exchanging ideas, noticing how the others respond, learn how to handle many situations.

Those who plan, design, build, and those who inhabit the neighbourhoods, should recognise qualities of traditional design elements of mohallas/wadas that could be employed for society's benefits. The issue is not, that in this day and age we should in every respect mimic/ replicate the past. It is that our historic communities embodied many important understandings about human nature, about what contributes to a satisfying individual and family life and a healthy society. The past does possesses an accumulation of wisdom which we ignore at our peril. The development patterns of most of Delhi's residential neighbourhoods make for an inconvenient way of living, one that generates a variety of troubles for the residents.

A good residential neighbourhood must be safe, clean and have adequate water supply, sanitary and storm drainage system, reliable power supply, efficient telecom system. Buildings should conform to building bye-laws; should have police and fire protection services and adequate garbage collection and disposal. Have access to good schools, primary health services, parks and off-street parking facilities.

Neighbourhood streets must be planned as a network of different experiences, other than just a system for automobile access to individual homes on the plots. Neighbourhood character comes from the shape of the street, the integration of parks and esplanades, and the different destinations visible on the axis of each road.

The neighbourhood plan must encourage people to walk or ride a bicycle, there must be vistas and architectural drama to keep the journey interesting, and the street environment is designed for pedestrians.

The neighbourhood plan must provide community facilities functionally located within the residential area, so as to allow direct access by car, bicycle and by foot on pedestrian circulation system; and must create hierarchical system of recreational spaces in conjunction with educational facilities, so that their use is maximised.

Traditional Neighbourhood Design

New Urbanism—This movement in America incorporates characteristics from older communities—Walkability, pedestrian-friendly scaling and mixed land uses, to enhance new ones. It is a movement fueled by a variety of sources. Disdain for sprawl, love of quaint downtown and the desire for simple, efficient small town life.

Across USA, the number of New Urbanist developments planned or under construction nearly doubled from 1996 to 1998, according to the "New Urban News". The Congress for the New Urbanism, a San Francisco based organisation of architects, planners, developers and government officials, believes the desire for dense, walkable neighbourhoods could grow 17 per cent by 2015. Also called neo-traditional housing, to create livable communities, street by street, neighbourhood by neighbourhood.

Americans became accustomed to sprawling suburbs, but now home buyers are discovering New Urbanist alternatives—small towns and down towns. New Urbanism concentrates on certain principles to enhance a community's efficiency, walkability and liability. These principles encompass regional policies, such as balancing jobs with housing and local architectural features, to design modern neighbourhoods with traditional feel.

Traditional neighbourhood design is a relatively new movement in America. It began in the 1980s when Florida real estate developer designed "Seaside", one of the first Traditional Neighbourhood Design solutions. The development captured the vibrancy of an all-American small town. People want to live in neighbourhoods where there is a corner store and they do not need to drive everywhere.

We need to rethink our planning ideas–we need to develop suburbs, that foster neighbourhood and public life. We must design suburbs in a way, that public areas throughout the neighbourhood are enjoyable to use, and are treated as important, congenial places. Instead of glorifying interior and private spaces, while leaving the public environment dominated by ugly facades, we need to reorient houses so that they dignify and enliven the places, where residents come in contact with one another.

In the existing residential neighbourhoods houses built on plots are being demolished and replaced with multi-storeyed apartments that behemoth as daunting as a cliff–it represents a huge leap in scale. The old houses cower beneath the new comers.

We have to restore the neighbourliness which has been lost in Delhi's suburban landscape. Design of a residential neighbourhood is not a mere subdivision of land into plots and streets. The suburbs need physical heart or core, something many of Delhi's suburbs and some of the inner city residential areas lack.

The post-independence suburban development is the driving force behind the decline of Delhi's traditional urban and small city life. These suburban residential areas have no identity or a sense of place. We must call for the return of a sense of community in our residential areas.

Developers, urban planners and urban designers must answer the call in practical and innovative ways.

Have architecture that respects human-scale, respects regional history and ecology. Traditional architecture has much to teach us about these imperatives, without prescribing nostalgic forms. Climate, responsive to design that honours the history and culture of a place, and combined with new technology and lead to innovative rather than imitative design.

Residential neighbourhoods can be shaped by choice or they can be shaped by chance. We either keep on accepting the kind of neighbourhoods we get, or we can insist on getting the kind of neighbourhoods we want. It was Sir Winston Churchill who said that "we shape our cities and then our cities shape us". The choice is ours whether we build sub-divisions that debase the human spirit or neighbourhoods that nurture sociability and bring out the best in our nature. The techniques for achieving the latter are well known, and available to all who wish to make places worth caring about.

It is the buildings–houses, that comprise a place, and architecture it is said, is the art of place making. We have not shaped our place in Delhi, residential or commercial in the post-independence era so well.

Traditional residential neighbourhoods that gave the inhabitants there a sense of belonging. Every residential area in the capital's suburbs is more like every other residential area, all adding up to no-place. The built spaces of the city deeply influence the quality of community life, therefore, the urban planners and architects have the responsibility to design and construct an aesthetically pleasing environment for the citizens of Delhi.

We need a society of neighbourhoods, a culture of personal responsibility. Today not much attention is given to management aspects of residential neighbourhoods. Unless our neighbourhoods are permanently managed by trained personnel, the best residential areas could be converted into slums. Good housing management is based on a developing social consciousness. Therefore, self-managed neighbourhoods must be undertaken to provide for their own welfare, through active and sustained community participation.

The Residential Welfare Associations (RWA) need to play a key role in revitalisation of residential neighbourhoods and for promoting a sense of community, supported by national resources. Neighbourhood-based initiatives are important, because they ensure that the residents both initiate and support programmes for their own neighbourhoods. Chances for success can improve dramatically, when the neighbourhood community is a partner to development.

To make Delhi a better place, we the citizens, must bring our new visions of development and policy goals to the local level, down to where people live, down to where they experience development, down to where people themselves take initiatives, to transform their own living conditions.

Residents' Welfare Associations must be empowered as new players in efforts to revitalise neighbourhoods on the decline. A community development movement is necessary. A movement that involves citizens participation and political commitment and government and private sector support for neighbourhood planning and development.

At the dawn of independence, Delhi's population was less than two million people, today Delhi has 15 million people, creating an entirely new scale of urban development, a scale that has changed the nature and character of urban form.

From the detached house, through semi-detached and attached row-house on plots to the apartment blocks and high-rise buildings, is the response of the inhabitants of Delhi to population pressure.

The problem of mega-scale is real. The land resources being severely restricted, high densities became inevitable. High rise residential buildings are being super imposed on plots in place of a detached or semi-detached house.

The mitigate the chaos that has created as a result, will require new inventions, new design methodologies, and unprecedented solutions. The architectural profession must rise to the occasion; the mega scale must be recognised as a paradigm shift that inevitably challenges the basic assumptions of architecture.

One of the most frustrating aspects of living in a high rise apartment building is its inaccessibility to the outdoors, like sitting in a garden.

However, architect Moshe Safdie's 'Habitat' which he designed and built at the Montreal Expo in 1967, emerged as a structure combining some of the amenities of single-family housing with the unique opportunities of a high-rise building. It substituted exterior walkways for interior corridors, shaping the building's mass to create roof-gardens, multiple exposures, acoustic privacy, and articulating the scale of individual dwellings.

As Habitat Complex was inhabited, a change in perception immediately occurred on the part of its residents: Corridor became street, apartment became house and balcony a garden. The pleasures of living in privacy were added to the benefits of living in close community. Increasingly, in the core as well as the perimeters of Delhi, for the poor, the middle-income, and the affluent, the high-rise apartment building emerges as the predominant urban form.

Gated Communities

Fear of crime and buglary and car-jacking has become a major social problem in the National Capital. The overall fear of crime is increasing. It has created a boom in the security service industry. Throughout the metropolis, there are a variety of types of protected areas, including individual houses with gates and a guard.

Delhiites are concerned about crimes and armed robberies, which is why they live behind high fences and gates, to ameliorate the impact of crime and violence in their daily lives.

The houses, roads, sidewalks and other amenities are physically enclosed by these barriers, and entrance gates are operated by guards. These gated residential areas restrict access, not just to residents' homes, but also to the use of public spaces and services—roads, parks and open spaces–contained within the enclosure.

(C) The Traffic Gridlock

Over the years, with growing population, Delhi has become a dispersed metropolis, and with its indispensible car, has created problems of mobility and parking.

Traffic is the first thing people notice about Delhi. Cars, scooters, motorbikes, autorickshaws and buses swarm the roads. They all operate according to a perverse rule of the road, that seem designed to cause accidents, not prevent them. Green light, red light, it does not matter. Drivers start or stop as they please. Vehicles swerve between lanes. The absence of traffic police and discipline is largely responsible for all the chaos on Delhi's roads.

For the majority of Delhiites, traffic jams and congested roads have become a way of life. As the capital's population has grown, so have the number of motor vehicles, at a far greater rate than new roads and urban highways are being added to the existing infrastructure. For the drivers of these vehicles, this has meant increasing frustration over delays and inconsistent commuting times. Increases in traffic congestion have outpaced attempts to expand Delhi's transportation infrastructure.

The state of the vehicular traffic in Delhi, is perhaps the most serious single problem, affecting the daily lives of the people in the nation's capital. Delhi a product of a long historic evolution, served only by some simple form of transportation, is now threatened with disintegration, by the invasion of motor vehicles, for which Delhi's road system was never designed in the first place. Today the motor vehicles are in conflict with the urban structure of Old and New Delhi, and the suburbs. This conflict appears very difficult to reconcile, because of the competing demand for urban space, for movement of vehicles, as well as, for parking.

Delhi's roads, particularly during rush hours are unable to accommodate the volume of traffic. Thus a half-an-hour trip from home to workplace takes anywhere between an hour or more. The physical conflict between the number of people desiring personal mobility and the capacity of the capital's road system to accommodate them is rapidly escalating.

The traffic problems, that Delhi faces, are so critical and exacerbating and rushing upon us with such speed, that it amounts to virtually an emergency. Problems such as traffic congestion, chaos and grid locks, leading to inordinate delays, accident and pollution, constitute serious threats to the continued economic health and public safety of this great metropolis–the Capital of India.

Anything goes on Delhi's roads. More than three million vehicles now choke the roads—private cars, motorcycles, scooters, taxis, autorickshaws, buses, overladen trucks, angrily sputtering from one lane to the next. Five persons die in traffic accidents everyday. The privately owned buses alone account for almost three hundred deaths a year. Often with untrained drivers at the wheel, urged on by conductors, desperate to sell more seats than their rivals, they race one another through the streets, routinely picking up and discharging passengers in mid-traffic. Delhi's traffic related death toll is higher than any other major city in India.

Because of ungovernable traffic, Delhi has become the world's fourth most polluted metropolis. Vehicles spew 1430 tons of exhaust fumes into the air everyday–enough to ring the inside of your nose with black carbon, within moments of leaving your house. One report estimates that the average Delhiites inhales daily, the toxic equivalent of the smoke from 20 cigarettes. Another report found that 7,500 people die from pollution related diseases each year, and four million more are treated for them at city hospitals.

For the millions of Delhiites, the daily journey-to-work, mostly in crowded buses, is a veritable nightmare ; battling their way through the traffic snarl at rush hours. The growing traffic problems, have placed in jeopardy the well-being of the people in Delhi, and so also the efficiency of many activities and delivery of services. Delhi metropolis has grown to the point whereby it threatens to chock the very motorised transportation that brought it into being. Under these conditions traffic has affected our lives by making us a restless and nervous race of people. We are all afflicted by "automania" an illness common to motor car dominated urban societies.

On the one hand, there is a policy to manufacture cars of different types. On the other, the city authorities are not concerned about providing capacity for movement of vehicles and for parking. Delhi's road capacity is grossly insufficient to carry the volume of traffic that the city generates. Congestion equals too many vehicles on too few lanes. The road capacity is further reduced by encroachments on road right-of-way, traffic bottlenecks at poorly designed intersections, on street parking, pedestrians movement and heterogeneity of traffic ; all these factors spell traffic jams and chaos. The traffic problem is further exacerbated by rash and negligent driving and the lack of enforcement of traffic laws and regulations. When the Delhi traffic police are unable to enforce traffic laws, disrespect for law and order grows and when our courts cannot enforce their decrees the process of law and order breaks down. The increase of motor vehicles, capable of high-speed, has on the contrary resulted in the progressive retarding of transportation and piling up costs.

The Municipal Corporation of Delhi is a self-government for local affairs of which city traffic and transportation forms a part, yet it is one of its most neglected functions. Responsibility for traffic operations is shifted entirely to the Delhi Police, who are part of the Central Home Ministry and not the city. In reality the police are concerned only with enforcement of traffic rules and regulations. The MCD is the one responsible for providing the necessary traffic infrastructure. Both the MCD and the Delhi Traffic Police conduct their respective activities, with rudimentary and peripheral knowledge of the subject of traffic engineering and traffic operations. It is a small wonder, that these organisations are unable to grapple with the proliferating traffic on Delhi's road network.

There is no comprehensive approach to dealing with urban traffic problems in Delhi, instead the concerned authority resorts to measures directed at finding spot solutions, which succeed only in shifting traffic congestion from one area of the city to another. Such solutions lack applicability in a wider context of overcoming the traffic problems on a long-term basis. Delhi has been resorting to costly improvements in road capacity just to keep traffic on the move, by building fly-overs at busy intersections, which as experience has shown, are unlikely to be of lasting benefit, since they are rapidly overtaken by the proliferating urban traffic. Besides, the fly-overs take the motorists more quickly from one traffic jam to another. Fly-overs have not solved the problem but instead compounded it. Inappropriate and unnecessarily expensive schemes like fly-overs, are destroying Delhi in the false name of resolving the traffic problems. More modest, appropriate and creative alternatives exist that could achieve the goals with minimal, if any, damage to the urban environment.

Fly-overs are built in Delhi without a clear understanding of the consequences. They may relieve circulation pressure on one side and create traffic congestion on another. They give relief to one section of Delhi and kill another. "Trying to cure traffic congestion by adding more capacity, is like trying to cure obesity by loosening your belt." The more facilities are provided for the motor car, the more cars appear. 'Traffic increases to fill in the available space'.

When most of the daily trips are performed on mass public transport in Delhi, it is counter productive to devise a structure for the metropolis on the basis that nearly all journeys will be made by individual modes like cars, motorcycles and scooters, oblivious of the fact that such a structure demands an investment in urban highways and grade separated intersections (fly-overs) so huge that the limited resources cannot possibly provide for it. Moreover, there is no space to provide roads for unlimited private mode of transportation in Delhi.

In a metropolis where only 15 per cent of the daily trips are made by cars and scooters/motorcycles, it makes no economic sense to spend such colossal amount of money on fly-overs. This cost should have been transferred to improving mass transit system, on which over 75 per cent of the trips are performed daily. Cost and problem of parking also could be minimised, when daily commuters use the mass transportation. Our short-term vision blinds us to the consequences of our actions. We are mortgaging the future for the present. But this is how the government bureaucracy functions, doing what is expedient and not what is necessary. In the process we are sacrificing all the special values of historic Delhi to the function of automobiles.

Looking at the complexity of urban traffic and transportation problems in Delhi, the Municipal government must eschew piecemeal and ad hoc measures and instead adopt a comprehensive and systems approach to deal with it. The potential increase in the number of motor vehicles in Delhi is so great that unless the powers-that-be act to deal with the problems, traffic may paralyse urban life very soon. The next several decades promise to be ones of growing congestion, financial crunch, dwindling energy resources, and mobility problems for most of the people of Delhi.

As a priority greater attention will have to be paid to improving the management and optimization of existing traffic capacity and developing viable public mass transit options, before getting into the preparation of a comprehensive Traffic and Transportation Plan as an integral part of the comprehensive development plan for the national capital.

Peter Wolf in his book "The Future of the City", writes: "To redesign cities to accommodate the car is to redesign cities out of existence. The car and the city are natural enemies. To experience the city, one must be able to participate in it, to walk the streets, take a public transport.

While motorised transportation is critical to any city in India, it is too important to be looked upon only as a method of moving people, goods and services. Urban transportation must be seen as a means of designing a more satisfactory urban environment. Because, much that would be done to improve the environment, would also help improve transportation. In fact this two-way relationship between transportation and the city-structure and form, could prove to be the key to urban revolution in India. It is essential, then, that we develop principles and techniques to link effectively the handling of motorised traffic with the designing or restructuring of the metropolis.

The Government of National Capital Territory must make all out effort to resolve the problem of mobility in the metropolis, by means other than by individually driven private cars, motorcycles and scooters. The greatest single challenge of dealing with urban transportation is of striking a balance between making the metropolis adapt to the demands of motorised traffic and at the same time of restoring and conserving the quiet tranquility which made earlier Delhi so liveable.

Decongestant Needed for Traffic Headaches

The most annoying consequence of the rapid growth of Delhi has been traffic, which continues to choke roads and nettle commuters, almost wherever they seem to turn. Delhi's roads and intersections are ill-equipped to handle modern big city traffic, making it the most bottlenecked city. Rush-hour traffic snarls at many intersections have become a major hardship for capital" travelling public, who certainly must wonder how much longer they will have to endure, before the authorities wake up and do something to alleviate the log jam.

As Delhiites rely more and more on their cars, scooters and motorbikes, as their primary mode of transportation, traffic congestion becomes more ubiquitous. Traffic jams are a waste of time and money. Dissecting why traffic jams occur, however, is harder than identifying how they occur. It is easy to pinpoint any number of causes of a traffic jam. Congestion is the obvious reason for traffic jams. For example to maintain a free flow of traffic on Delhi's streets, with their operating speed at about 10 to 15 km. per hour, there can be no more than 200 cars per lane per hour. More than that will tax the street's capacity and translate to more traffic jams. When additional vehicles try to get on to an already congested street that creates an interruption that affects cars up the stream of traffic. The crawling traffic in the Nation's Capital is causing huge financial loss to the nation. During rush hours of morning and evening fuel worth over Rs. 24 crore annually of (248 working days) is burnt on each of Delhi's 20 major intersections stops. Long traffic hold-ups are also resulting in massive loss of man-hours. About 1,300 crore man-hour lost annually. It is the poor traffic management that is leading to unnecessary burning of fuel where stopping time is between 10 to 15 minutes.

Driving, which once was a great pleasure, today is dangerous. Many drivers either do not know or neglect to use some of the basic safety rules of driving–the use of turn signals and lane-change indicators. Aggressive driving has become a danger that sometimes leads to 'road rage'. The traffic in Delhi is getting worse all the time. It's going to get to the point where travelling by car to work just won't be possible.

I read about Bangkok described as a rich city but poor life. Due to traffic jams, some of the drivers won't leave home without a mobile phone. Bangkok is a city of 10 million or more people with so little central planning that up until the late 1990s it had no rapid transit system. Bangkok stopped entertaining on week nights because of the uncertainty of when guests would arrive.

Traffic congestion takes a toll on more than just the behind-the-wheel psyche. There is a cost on traffic congestion in terms of lost hours of worker productivity and wasted litres of fuel burnt away while idling in traffic. The cost is greatest for those who live in far-flung suburbs of Delhi. Alleviating traffic congestion, has the potential to reduce critical airborne pollutants, by million of tons each year, while adding economic benefits to the nation. Reducing delays, has a direct effect on the reduction of greenhouse gases. The longer the cars and other vehicles sit in traffic, the more pollutants they emit. Smoothing traffic flows at chock-points, would help lower carbon dioxide emissions on vehicles travelling through the bottlenecks. Fossil fuels (petrol or diesel) consumed by Delhi's motor-vehicles produce chlorofluro carbons, methane and nitrogen oxides that trap heat and raise the temperature in the metropolis. Winter smog at nights makes driving virtually impossible and hazardous.

Traffic Management

The authorities that are supposed to be dealing with traffic and transportation in the capital, are not realising the advantages of making optimum use of existing system capacity, through traffic engineering, improved mass transportation and road pricing policy techniques. The technology that is appropriate for bringing relief to Delhi's proliferating traffic problem is the establishment of Transportation System Management, which aims at the optimisation of Delhi's existing road network capacity, mass transportation services, plus other related facilities. The concept of TSM is to view all elements of urban transportation–public and private as parts of a single system, organised and operated with appropriate traffic regulations and pricing policies. The approach would be to combine the pricing of automobiles use and parking with preferential use of roads by mass transport buses, and control over automobile use during the rush hours.

The objective of TSM is of coordinating all types of private motor vehicles, mass transportation buses, MRTS, bicycles and pedestrians, which constitute urban traffic, in the metropolis of Delhi, through operational, regulatory and service policies, for achieving maximum efficiency and productivity as a whole. The idea is to redress the balance between short-term and long-term planning and encourage more efficient use of existing transport resources that Delhi has.

Transport System Management actions include, a broad range of measures, designed to obtain optimum use of road space for vehicular traffic, improve mass transportation service by buses, and alter travel demand. The actions also include, traffic engineering for improving the traffic geometry of the major intersections, road use priorities parking management, staggering of working-hours, and pricing incentives and disincentives.

As is being done in some cities of the world, Delhi too must find some method of deliberately limiting the number of private cars in the busy and crowded central and other business districts like Connaught Place and Chandni Chowk. either by licensing or by some form of taxation. Charging private cars the extra cost incurred by the city to furnish them with street capacity during rush hours is one way to bring about a more equitable use of street space. People who drive in their private cars on crowded city roads during rush hours are costing the city much more than they pay in any form of taxation. If they are required to pay out of their own pockets for the cost of congestion, they would jolly-well leave their cars behind at home.

Tax on Driving in the City Centre

Levying a charge for cars wishing to enter Connaught Place or any other similar busy congested commercial area, at particular times of the day, known as road pricing or congestion pricing has been in use in several cities in the world. Such a measure becomes necessary to affect change in the behaviour of car drivers, and to cut back on the extent to which urban space is taken over by the car. The resultant funds generated be invested in mass public transportation. For road pricing to be effective requires improvements in public mass transit. Cars entering CP and other similar centres, during the congested peak hours would be charged a fee. Sole purpose is to reduce congestion during peak hours. The price of travelling should be higher at the places and times of day when demand for (and benefit from) using them is greatest.

London Mayor Ken Livingstone's determination to press ahead with a radical proposal to reduce traffic congestion in Central London, could become a model for other crowded cities around the world. The proposal contains an imposition of daily tax of $7.15 on every driver who enters Central London between 7 a.m. and 7 p.m. on weekdays. There will be digital cameras, static and mobile, to read license plates and check against a database of vehicles for which the tax has been paid. Violators will be fined $57, rising to $171 if they fail to pay on time.

The Mayor's plan would reduce traffic in Central London, by as much as 15 per cent, a city of over 7 million people, and force thousands of motorists onto buses and subway trains, and cut air pollution. The Mayor has the backing of the British Government, the Confederation of British Industry and London First, a business group. One million people work in Central London, and 1 in 7 commute by car. Singapore and Oslo operate similar programmes.

No one doubts that London's traffic congestion is spiraling out of control and its public transport system is troubled. The poor state of the subway system is one argument against the traffic-reduction scheme. The public transport system is pretty well falling apart, and more problems will be created if they push more people onto it before improving it. The Mayor's proposal will simply push traffic problems out of the city centre and onto the periphery. There would be chaos at the edge of the exclusion zone as drivers try to park or find ways around the zone, for which London's ring road does not have the capacity to handle the added traffic.

That is why Delhi must introduce a system of licenses and prohibitions, so that only a minority of private cars or truck traffic are permitted access to crowded Connaught Place, and other similar crowded centres during rush hours. Establishing car-restricted zones in Connaught Place for instance where the cars operate so inefficiently due to congestion, and converting selected streets for pedestrians and bicycles would be a little loss for the motorists and a boom to pedestrians and merchants and traders. Delhi has far greater need to provide such facilities for those who walk or ride bicycles to work, whose number is very large. Either of these measures need to be simultaneously accompanied with great improvement and expansion in mass public transportation. Buses would carry many more commuters at the same cost if the roads were less crowded.

The Central Government's Ministry for Urban Development, a nodal Ministry for urban transportation, ought to play its legitimate role assigned to it. The Ministry should give financial grants to the major cities in India, through the State Governments, for preparing plans for an integrated system of urban transportation, setting out how they propose to handle their traffic and transportation problems both on short-term and long-term basis. The Ministry must ensure that when Delhi and other cities prepare comprehensive city development plans, traffic and transportation plan should be made an integral part of the overall plan for the development of the metropolis. At present the Master Plans contain land use policy, but no urban transportation policy. Simply blue-printing a future major road-network and mass transit routes on land use plan is not a transportation policy. We have the most behind-the-years retrograde urban planning in Delhi, because we separate land use planning from transportation planning.

We need to get a better understanding of the functional relationship between land use (activities on land) and transportation (traffic). Because traffic is a function of land use, which means that various kinds of activities in the city based on land, generate different types of volume of traffic. It is essential, therefore, to gain more knowledge, through urban traffic studies, of the precise nature of the relationship between land use and transportation and about the extent of their mutual effect.

There are two fundamental issues in contemporary urban planning–urban environment and transportation. Environment has precedence over transportation, because the ultimate goal of urban planning is to improve the conditions and quality of urban life. The emphasis, therefore, is on improving the living conditions in our cities, to envision the urban future that was in our ability to achieve and to use the tools of urban planning, science and technology to make cities better places to live in.

Urban transportation is too important, to be seen simply as a means of moving traffic on city's roads. Transportation should be considered as a means of designing a more satisfying urban environment, in the process urban mobility would well be served. Because much that would be done to improve the urban environment would also help improve transportation. This two-way relationship between transportation and urban structure could prove to be the key to the success of urban revolution in India. The bottom line is, instead of trying to force the fabric of the city to fit traffic, as we are doing now, we must make all out effort to device means of transportation to fit the city. Europeans have intelligently developed small cars that fit admirably into a tight urban pattern of their cities.

Public Mass Transportation

Years ago, designing a bus service that connected people to jobs was not so difficult. The jobs were in the core of the city. The people were in suburbs. As new jobs moved to the suburbs, bus routes were slow to adapt to the changing needs of bus riders, who found that the system no longer met their needs. Travel pattern have changed with all the new businesses and residential development.

The high cost of individual transportation, plus the practical, economic and physical impossibility of approximately duplicating the space, required by each individual mode, by an equal space for parking mode, by an equal space for parking his car, motorcycle or scooter, makes mass transportation essential.

With shortsighted and uncoordinated mass transportation, it is time to look into each component of capital's urban transportation, the relationships and interfaces between them, and their link to the quality of the urban environment we live in. No single method as the break through to an effortless commute. Car-oriented development demands of urban highways, fly-overs, roads and parking facilities.

The present overcrowded and obsolete forms of mass transportation in Delhi constitutes a major problem for commuters. The unpleasantness as well as the time required for the journey-to-work, is one reason why commuters have turned to individual mode of transportation. Therefore, we must make mass transit a more attractive and viable alternative to driving. If not, the motorists, we can lure convenience happy scooter and motorcycle drivers, at least on to mass transit.

Vitality of the Delhi metropolis depends on the adequacy and efficiency of the road and traffic system, therefore, the creation of a system capable of coping with the demands of modern traffic, must be taken note of as a primary feature in a comprehensive urban plan for the nation's capital. Undoubtedly, the task ahead is staggering, because the traffic problems have developed much more rapidly than the techniques for their solution, because the costs are tremendous, and because, even while improvements are in process, the problems continue to grow beyond calculations. Traffic problems grows faster than palliative can be applied.

The Colling Buchanan Report on "Traffic in Towns" states, that a city can only be made to function efficiently and provide a decent environment for living, by giving a new dynamic role to our mass public transportation. In Delhi it is more relevant because over 60 per cent of the total person trips per day are made by mass transportation, such as buses and commuter trains. Private modes like cars, motorcycles, scooters cater to the smallest per centage of person trips and yet utilize most of urban space for their movement and parking. Buses in Delhi which cater to a higher proportion of passenger trips, get relatively little space, and the pedestrians often the largest part of the city traffic, invariably are marginalised, when it comes to providing pedestrian paths.

Top priority should be given to mass transportation rather than to individual mode of transportation, and to pedestrians rather than to motor vehicles. Bicycle paths and pedestrian walkways should be an integral part of the road network and public transportation system in the Capital.

Sixty persons in a bus use a lot less fuel and cause much less pollution than the same number of persons in private cars which also need parking space. Intra-city traveller facing the choice between using his private car or scooter or motor-bike and mass transportation will be influenced in his choice more by the passenger comfort, speed, frequency of service, a reasonable price, than by the distance he must travel in his own vehicle or by local transit to reach the nearest rapid transit station.

We must make mass public transportation an attractive alternative to the travel by individual private mode, the type that lure commuters out of their cars, motorcycles and scooters to mass transit system. It has to be demonstrated to the travelling public, that mass transit is not just for those who cannot afford cars, scooters or motorcycles. This underscores that the city has to provide a mass transit system, that demonstrably competes with individual mode of transportation in efficiency, comfort and safety as well as reliability. Unless we recognise the importance of mass transportation for Delhi, parts of the metropolis which is already being destroyed to make way for traffic will be further get pulled down in an attempt to get rid of traffic congestion, and at the end find that congestion still remains while the character of the metropolis destroyed.

Daily Journey-to-Work

Every Delhiites finds his or her daily journey-to-work abhorring. Indeed, their complaints sound familiar to anyone, who has stewed in frustration in a car or bus, crawling at a mile or less an hour, behind a seemingly endless line of cars, buses, scooters, three-wheelers, trucks and what have you, down a seemingly endless stretch of roads. We all hate the rush hour. We complain and put up with traffic jams. What choice do we have?

While the majority of Delhi's population is dependent on mass public transportation, the Delhi's transport authority has not given any serious consideration, to developing a mass transit system, that would be more efficient than the present bus system, but instead the Delhi government builds urban highways and fly-overs for the use of private motor vehicles driven by fewer number of people and in the process they are destroying the physical environment of the city. Government's short-sighted policy gives relief to immediate problems while creating profound ones. Jam-packed buses, uncomfortable ride, long wait at bus stops, buses moving at a slow speed, due to street congestion. Most travelling public depends on bus service, which are badly maintained, shabby condition of buses, give appearance of moffisil bus service.

There is something about the buses in Delhi people dislike. They feature the fewest cubic feet of elbow room per passenger. Because they have to make so many stops, and frequently have round about routes, they are often slower even than bumper-to-bumper traffic, during rush hours. The authorities in Delhi have sacrificed every other form of urban transportation to private automobiles. The flyovers are a symbol of enthroning the automobile. A city exists, not for the constant passage of motor cars, but for the care and culture of humanity (urbanites).

A stable solution to urban transportation in the capital, is possible only if we give due weightage to all the necessary elements in transportation–private car, railways, mass transportation by buses and MRTS, and not least, the pedestrian. We just cannot have one-dimensional transportation system by automobiles alone. Each mode of transportation has its special use, and an intelligent urban transportation policy for the Capital, should be towards improving each type and make the optimum use of it.

To become a world class metropolis, the Capital of a great nation, Delhi needs a superior mass transit system. The economy is hurt, if people in Delhi cannot get where they need to go. Using public transportation conserves energy and preserves our environment, so every one can enjoy the great outdoors. This is the only environmentally friendly way of enhancing urban mobility. It is tough to get people out of their cars. Mass transit system has to be easy to navigate, have one fare structure, and be attractive, from the cleanliness of the vehicles to the friendliness of the conductors and drivers. Creation of a single ticket system allows riders to use all modes of public transit– the bus, the MRTS and the railway.

Integrated Transport System

In the absence of an adequate and integrated public transportation system, daily commuters in the nation's capital depend on private mode of transportation. Whether it's a journey-to-work, a business trip or else, when we have an integrated road-and-rail system in place, the commuter can first hop on to a bus from the point of origin, then get on to a metro at the MRTS station, get off the metro train and board a bus again to destination. Chances are, that it will drop you off right at your workplace. The MRTS which runs along high density corridors, need interlinks with residential and commercial hubs and major work-centres, like the Central Secretariat Complex for instance. The existing city-bus routes should be modelled so that they become feeders to MRTS, instead of replicating the same routes.

In Delhi, no other phase of urban services is handled by so many different agencies, as vehicular traffic, city bus and MRTS, and no other phase receives as little attention in scientific and traffic engineering planning. To deal effectively and comprehensively with capital's traffic and transportation problems, it is essential to establish a single command, under a Metropolitan Transport Authority, to ensure planning, coordination, budgeting, programming and phasing of projects and modernising Delhi's traffic operations and providing an integrated mass transportation system and off-street parking for cars.

Road Intersections

There are certain aspects of road planning that merit special consideration. One of them is road intersection. In Delhi most of the road intersections are a sore spots. They limit the traffic capacity of roads and are the locus of most of road accidents.

The poorly designed or not designed at all road intersections in the Capital put a restraint on the safe and smooth flow of traffic on major roads. The traffic capacity of a road is no greater than the traffic capacity of its intersections. Therefore, the intersection design or the traffic geometries have to take into consideration, the multi-directional interchange of vehicles at an intersection.

Intersection design must provide for the channelisation of left and right turning traffic, as well as for traffic moving ahead. In the absence of channelisation, there is traffic-scramble at the intersections leading to delays and accident hazards.

A fundamental requisite of a safe intersection is adequate vision clearance, so that drivers of vehicles approaching the intersection have an uninterrupted view in all directions, before he enters it.

In residential areas, this can be secured by requiring houses on corner plots, to be setback from the road line on both the front and side roads, and by prohibiting high walls, fences or hedges, that would obstruct the view.

Adequate street lighting is a valuable safeguard against traffic accidents, especially at the intersections. There seems to be no realisation of this very important aspect of road planning in Delhi.

The design of street lighting facilities is a highly specialised science. Street lighting requirements vary with the different areas of Delhi residential, business and industrial with the different kinds of roads in each of these areas. Major and minor roads, and with difference in the width, and planting along them.

A comprehensive survey of the metropolis of Delhi should be made to determine where new lights to be installed and installations replaced, and the programme should then be carried out on a definitely established basis of priority.

Parking

There is scarcely a business and shopping area in the capital that is not handicapped by a lack of an adequate amount of parking facilities. And yet, no one has found a single, simple solution for the parking problem that the people of Delhi face.

In the absence of off-street parking facilities such as parking lots, multilevel parking garages, the motor vehicles are seen parked on the road-kerbs, which materially reduces the traffic carrying capacity of the road, to as much as fifty per cent.

Therefore, kerb-parking needs to be regulated. Kerb-parking should be prohibited during rush hours so as to provide optimum utilisation of road capacity. When kerb parking is permitted during off-peak hours, it must be on the basis of limited parking, ranging from one to two hours, to be regulated along the kerbs.

An eventual step must be to prohibit parking in congested areas like Connaught Place, Chandni Chowk and the like, for a time longer than necessary for transacting business or shopping and for freight vehicle for loading and unloading. However, this can only be achieved after adequate off-street parking facilities are in place.

But the space available for off-street parking is limited to cater to ever-increasing demand for parking in already congested business districts of Delhi. The pressure on available parking spaces can be relieved to the extent that commuters to these areas are persuaded to use mass transportation facilities, rather than private mode of travel. But here again the mass transportation system must be made, reliable and efficient enough to attract passengers travelling by private cars.

Environment Friendly Bicycle

During the preparation of the first-ever Master Plan for Delhi in the late 1950s, the traffic survey indicated that there were about 7 lac bicycles in Delhi. Most of the cyclists rode on the streets, for want of separate bicycles tracks. Hence, express bicycle tracks were proposed in the Delhi Master Plan, 1981 indicating their alignments on the land use plan map. Like many others, this proposal too, like many others never got on the ground.

Bicycles have several attractions for the user. For one thing he is not expending money on fares or fuel. The bicycle provides the user with excellent physical exercise, recommended by doctors for strengthening the healthy heart. Bicycle take up relatively little space, create no traffic jams, or pollute the air with fumes and noise, and a cyclist is unlikely to cause any damage to pedestrians. On the positive side the cyclist has advantages over the car driver, being above the car and being unenclosed, he has all-round vision.

The cyclist has a non-stop door-to-door journey, which the car driver often spends some time looking for a parking slot. He can ride through red-light and difficult intersections, and pass traffic jams. In fact for short trips, particularly those involving several separate stops for shopping, and so on, the cyclist takes little longer than a car and experiences none of the car driver's frustration.

In Delhi, we have forgotten or ignored this relatively low-tech mobility option. It is time to improve bicycle facilities and enhance bicycle safety by creating city-wide bicycle network of express tracks. A number of European Cities have taken steps to substantially limit automobile traffic in their centres. Some cities have converted their centres to car-free district, limited to bicycles and pedestrians and public transit. There is a network known as "Car Free Cities" based in Brussels of about 60 cities, working on these issues. Many participating cities have signed the Copenhagen Declaration, making a commitment to finding ways, to reduce the pressure of automobiles in their cities.

4

Planning Initiative

Town planning is a professional discipline, which originated in the early decades of the Twentieth Century in response to public concern over the deteriorating social and economic conditions created by industrialisation.

Town planning had its beginning in Delhi, when Sir Edwin Lutyen planned and designed the city of New Delhi as the Capital of the British Empire in the early Twentieth Century. The ownership of all land, including that developed by the private sector, was retained by the British Government. Under such ideal conditions, development of Delhi ought to have proceeded along sound planning principles, and in an integrated manner. But it had not been so, not because of lack of necessary powers, but more so because of the failure to coordinate policies among different agencies of the government, involved in land development.

Even after official opening of New Delhi Capital in 1931, nothing had been done to integrate Paharganj, Old Delhi, the old city's extension to the west, and Shahdara across the river Yamuna. Progressively, problems of the old city and its extensions, continued to grow worse, and occasionally drew the attention of government. In 1936, A.P. Hume Report on 'Relief of Congestion in Delhi', led to creation of Delhi Improvement Trust in 1937. It was formed to tackle limited range of urban problems in Delhi. Delhi Improvement Trust was thus added to the multiplicity of local bodies, which by 1950 included Delhi Municipal Committee, New Delhi Municipal Committee, the Notified Area Committee, the Civil Lines, as well as Central Government's the Land Development Officer and the Central Coordinating Committee for Greater Delhi established in 1948.

Massive migration of refugees 500,000 or more to Delhi, subsequent to Independence and Partition in August 1947, called for emergency action. Housing, feeding and employing a gigantic numbers, were sometimes chaotic and involved compromises on standards and intelligent urban planning. Awareness of these problems, prompted Government of India to appoint in April 1950, Delhi Improvement Trust Enquiry Committee, under the Chairperson Birla, which focused not only on the working of the Trust, but also on the deteriorating situation in the urban area of Delhi. In May 1951, the Birla Committee published its findings, in a two-volume Report.

The Report noted that the achievements of the DIT during the thirteen years of its existence are not at all impressive. The Trust had undertaken neither a Civic Survey nor Master Plan, with the result the growth of Delhi has been proceeding in a haphazard manner, with little foresight and imagination and without any coordination.

However, the Report noted that in fairness to the Trust's problem in carrying out its work, it had been called upon to deal with responsibilities that were unprecedented, had to bear expenses that ought not to have been its responsibility, and was only one of several agencies such as the Land and Development Department, the Central Public Works Department, and the Ministry of Rehabilitation, entrusted with development matters.

The Birla Committee made suggestions about control of both government and private development projects, and recommended a central authority to make planning schemes and administer them with adequate powers. The Committee emphasised that conflicting and overlapping jurisdictions be untangled under one autonomous planning authority. Thus, the Delhi Development (Provisional) Authority came into being in 1955. In December of the same year, the Central Government's Ministry of Health established the Town Planning Organisation, as an advisory body to the DD(P)A to prepare a Master Plan for Delhi.

Prior to the preparation of the Master Plan, the TPO prepared the Interim General Plan in September 1956. The purpose of IGP was to buy time until a comprehensive plan could be prepared. Though the IGP covered mainly the core area rather than the total of "greater Delhi", yet it emphasised the necessity of planning on a regional basis and the formation of a National Capital Region Authority; deconcentration of population; achieving a balanced distribution of land uses; reduction of journey-to-work by balanced distribution of work centres, accessible by better transportation facilities. Extensive attention was paid to public transportation, and the possibilities of staggering of work hours, to minimise rush hour traffic.

The Interim General Plan for Delhi was presented to Prime Minister Nehru's Cabinet members. The presentation was initiated by Raj Kumari Amrit Kaur,

Minister of Health and Local Self-government, assisted by some members of the TPO's planning Team. Raj Kumari was appreciative of the hard work and rare devotion to duty in producing the IGP in a remarkably short time, by the enthusiastic and competent body of Town Planners. She remarked "To build the India of our dreams is a great venture, and in its own way to rebuilt Our Capital City is also an exciting venture and if all will cooperate, the success of our plans is ensured".

The author was one of the member of the Delhi Master Plan, 1962 team headed by Architect-Planner, Shivnath Prasad. The team was privileged to have the consultancy services of a multi-disciplinary group of experts from America provided by the Ford Foundation's technical assistance programme.

The drafter Master Plan for Delhi-1962 prepared in the early 1960 was exhibited at the Vigyan Bhawan for presentation to Prime Minister Jawaharlal Nehru. Various elements of the Plan were explained to the PM by each member of the planning team. Nehru himself a planner and a visionary was visibly impressed and filled with excitement with the graphic presentation. Nehru was so enthused with the Draft Plan that he suggested the exhibition be opened to the Press, as well as to the visiting Pakistani delegation led by Gen. Yahya Khan and representatives of Doxiades whose firm was commissioned to plan the new Capital of Pakistan at Islamabad.

To Nehru, the Delhi Master Plan, 1962 being the very first comprehensive plan for guiding the development of the dynamic national capital of a new born nation was the beginning of comprehensive urban planning. It is said that P.M. Nehru in his regular letters to the Chief Minister of the States he addressed the importance of planning in regulating the growth of cities, which ultimately led to every State government enacting Town and Country Planning Acts for their respective States.

Experience has shown that for urban planning to be effective requires political patronage at the highest level, to that of the Chief Minister. Today it is just the contrary. Urban Planning has been marginalised both at the Centre and the States whereby laisser-fair approach to development prevails.

With the completion of the IGP, the process of planning for the whole of Delhi urban area was set in motion.

The Delhi Master Plan completed in early 1960s, was a pioneering effort of preparing a comprehensive, long-range, general plan for the capital of independent India, by a team of young planners, trained mainly in the United States of America, and the UK.

The specific issues, the Master Plan for Delhi addressed, was the ordering of the future of the capital for the maximum benefits of its residents, as well as the visitors. The basic pattern of scheme of the Plan, was to form all new developments and reform old ones, on the basis of a relatively self-contained unit, for meeting the daily needs, like employment, shopping, health and education, recreation and cultural facilities. The District Centre recommended, such as Nehru Place, was to be the nucleus of the unit with population ranging from 1 lakh to 1.5 lakh. This locational relationship was of overriding importance, in substantially minimising the demands on the costs of transportation and urban roads, both the capital as well as recurring maintenance costs.

Some of the most important goals the Plan aimed at was :

- for the best possible location of employment centres and housing, by optimum distribution of work places easily accessible to employees ;
- eradication of slums and shanty towns by providing adequate housing and related community facilities and services ;
- developing adequate mass transportation facilities and creating separate bicycle-express ways ;
- rebuilding deteriorated areas of the capital and application of effective regulations for new development ;
- combining utilitarian solutions to development problems with urban design for aesthetic effect ;
- assigning priorities to different projects and preparing programmes for their execution ; and
- analysis of costs for solving planning problems, the sources of funds needed to carry them out, and phasing and scheduling of the work by fiscal programme and capital budgeting.

The Delhi Master Plan emphasised that the balanced, comprehensive plan is impossible to achieve, unless all of the goals were met. Therefore, great care had to be exercised to make sure, that these goals were given highest priority, and were to be so phased in their execution, that they were consistent with financial and other resources, that would be made available. The great benefit of such a procedure is that no matter how little or how much can be undertaken in a particular period, what is done, fits into a long run plan and becomes organic rather than haphazard.

Planners that prepared the Master Plan for Delhi, being trained in USA and UK, applied considerable experience the Western World has had with urban planning, in addressing the planning problems of Delhi. However, transferring such experience, turned out to be limited. Planners need to find their own solutions to Delhi's urban problems. Despite the fact that cities everywhere have much in common, a fresh and innovative approach must be taken. The pressure of events at the time of preparing the Delhi Master Plan, made it difficult to learn from the shortcomings of western urban planning.

There is fundamental difference between the West and India, in the potential effectiveness of the whole Master Plan approach, as a primary step towards urban improvement. Because any such plan must take a great deal for granted, to begin with, since it is essentially a method of fitting together, a set of basic assumptions–the social and civic standards, into a complex physical scheme.

In most of the US and UK cities, these underlying assumptions and standards, were usually quite well understood then, and therefore, widely accepted. It was implicit in their master plans, that certain minimum physical standards of housing and services were both desirable and feasible, that growth trends could readily be projected and that the established economic base of the city, will continue to provide, both increased employment and adequate tax resources, with little direct public intervention, beyond zoning and services.

In India, the fundamental economic, social and demographic assumptions had hardly begun to be clarified then, in terms of viable urban standards. The planners also needed to ask, what the affordable overhead investment per capita be, say for the next 5 million urbanites in Delhi. Whatever the amount, how could it best be spent, to provide tolerable urban living conditions ! What should the optimum urban pattern be, from the viewpoint of social conditions, urban overhead costs, and maximum productivity in variable local conditions? No answers to such questions were available to the Planning Team then.

The Delhi Master Plan team had, therefore, simply to make some assumptions of their own, which may have turned out totally incorrect. Yet the Delhi Master Plan, 1962 provided a far better guide for urban development, than none at all, and also helped key issues. There is no such thing as perfect foresight; we can never plan infallibly, but we can face the urban future of Delhi with modesty and an approach tempered by a knowledge of earlier successes and failures. In order to understand where we are going, it is necessary to know where we have been.

It is essential for us to understand not only how to avoid repeating terrible mistakes of the past, but also how to recover from them. There is no final word or answer on what is the best way forward. We need to continue learning the lessons as they emerge.

Looking back, the Master Plan, 1962 approach had certain inherent limitations, which suggest that it was not the right one for situation prevailing in Delhi. One obvious fact is that it took years to produce any visible results, even in paper form. Delhi Plan took over six years, and equally long to get the plan sanctioned by the Government of India.

Another equally evident is the fact that the Delhi Plan was prepared by a Central Government Agency, the TPO, with no real powers of implementation.

A third limitation is its treatment of single urbanising area–Delhi, as an island, with little attention to national aspects or regional inter-relationships, which may be particularly important in India, a country with limited resources and most of its urban growth yet to come.

At this juncture, it is necessary to point out that having initially arrived at proposals for these needs in the Master Plan, the Master Plan studies ought to have been continued and actual conditions checked, against the projection of the Plan. Continued studies and thought, ought to have been directed, towards further planning, partly to keep in motion the implementation of the Master Plan, and partly to make any adjustments that become necessary, as new factors emerged to affect the national capital. None of this was done by the DDA, the sole Planning Authority, who had been charged with the responsibility of guiding the development of the capital according to the Master Plan. In fact the DDA's interest was more to exercise development controls and public works, rather than attempting at achieving the goals laid down in the Master Plan.

As per the Delhi Development Act, the Master Plan was to be reviewed every five years. Such a periodic review gives an opportunity to the Planning Authority to identify, where the reality corresponded with what was actually planned for Delhi, and indicate, where the reality deferred from what was planned. The DDA failed to evaluate why the differences had occurred, and to indicate those aspects of the Plan that were clearly in need of revision. The feedback from such an evaluation, would have helped, to influence the policy, and objectives for the future development of Delhi. It is very important, to constantly update the urban plan for Delhi.

The first ever Master Plan for Delhi (1962), even though thoughtfully made, became obsolete. The failure to plan for the current needs of Delhi, it must be recognised, that the planners could not possibly have foreseen the powerful and pervasive forces of urban growth and technology.

Reasons for the conflicts in the objectives of the plan are readily apparent. In the first place, the rate of urban growth in Delhi has been spectacular. Such a spectacle of urbanization was unprecedented. It came almost too fast for thought and certainly too rapidly for adequate foresight.

A weakness of urban planning in Delhi, was the failure of DDA, which had the custody of the Delhi Master Plan (1981), to see that it was not all embracing. As changes took place in technology, in standards of urban living, in the scope of city government (MCD), and in city planning generally, the planners in DDA failed to re-examine the Master Plan and to keep abreast of the times. The life of a city, like the life of a biological system, is continuous ; and action related to its development should be conceived as a continuous process. Therefore, the Delhi Master Plan and detail plans and programmes thereafter have to take this continuance into consideration.

Urban Planning Process

Planning urban development is a process and not an event or a final state brought to a halt by a master plan. Urban planning is a continuous, coordinative and programmatic process of engendering the development of the growing city. The operation of the urban planning process is a continuum of preparation of the plan, its sanctioning and finally its implementation.

Insofar as the preparation of the plan is concerned, although the DDA is a sole statutory planning authority, there are several public agencies in the national capital such as the NDMC, MCD, Power Company, DTC, Delhi State PWD and the like, whose activities significantly affect the development of Delhi urban area. Therefore, they are in effect plan preparation entities, and thus, have a vital role in the Delhi's urban development process.

Planning clearly has value. This is how the urban planning process operates :

> For its own activities, each agency in charge of water supply, electricity, public bus transport, roads, assesses its resources and projects, its services, and urban improvement and development programmes. Plan making by these specialised agencies has certain advantages ; it is done by persons expert in the techniques of the agency's programmes, it is done in close awareness of the needs of the agency and it tends to be practical, because it is usually influenced by the awareness of the problems of implementation.
>
> However, such plan making is by itself inadequate for dealing with the complex problems

of city development as a whole. Necessarily, each agency plans only for its own functions. Furthermore, single agency lacks the power to influence the plans of other agencies in Delhi, and some agencies may not have the staff or resources to prepare long-range plans.

This underscores the fact that technical expertise does not necessarily imply planning expertise also. As a result, planning by these agencies has to be accompanied by plan making at a higher level.

The DDA as the designated planning and development authority for Delhi is charged with the preparation of an overall plan for guiding development and redevelopment of the national capital, revising and adjusting where necessary, each agency's plans. This requires a close and continuous coordination of work between DDA and the various agencies.

Unfortunately, such an arrangement does not form part of the established urban planning system adopted in Delhi, although it is important that the DDA should have systematic means of getting full information on the plans of the other agencies and a method of adjusting their plans to its own and vice versa.

This can be accomplished only by incorporating into Delhi Development Act, the process known as 'Mandatory Referral', by virtue of which each agency is mandated to refer its plans to DDA to ensure conformity with the planning policy, principles and standards.

The Delhi Development Act and therefore the DDA on the contrary isolates the elements of the planning process, since it fails to provide the necessary linkages between plan preparation by various agencies in Delhi. Under the Act only DDA has any part in the preparation of the overall plan for Delhi.

Had DDA coordinated plan preparation by various agencies, it follows that it would also be required to coordinate the implementation of their plans. Because only DDA as a central agency can have the perspective, to oversee the entire implementation process, and provide direction and guidance, within the framework of the mutually agreed overall Master Plan and other plans. Therefore, the means and devices of cooperation essential to coordination at the plan preparation stage are equally essential for implementation.

Urban planning in Delhi has been regarded, solely in terms of preparing a master plan, by mapping the physical features of a possible future Delhi metropolis to succeed the present one. Planners shifted their interest away from determining physical form. They have become less attentive to whether the physical environment itself was being shaped adequately. This is the urban planning system operating under the Delhi Development Act, which lays emphasis on the preparation of Master Plan as the principal activity of urban development.

Experience has shown that the Master Plan with its rigid land use pattern, zoning and development controls, has proved extremely poor instruments for guiding and directing the dynamic process of urban growth and change that we see taking place in Delhi. There are no goals, such as, urban transport policy, structure of Delhi, or neighbourhood concept.

Inspite of DDA, which was especially set up for promoting and securing development of Delhi according to a Plan, planning has failed to improve living conditions and the quality of life in the capital city. Urban planning system in operation, is at best fragmented, uncoordinated, and at worst, basically non-existent and anarchic. Planning is administered by a bureaucratic planning authority, a negative force with executive powers of refusal and delay, without any accountability and entirely lacking the will or the resources, professional and financial, to take creative steps to make Delhi a more environment friendly city.

Urban planning does not end with the preparation of a Master Plan. Planning is a process and not an event. It is a continuous process of making a plan and getting it sanctioned and implementing it within a time frame. Planning at urban level must serve the needs and aspirations of the Delhiites. For urban planning to establish its credibility and gain recognition of the politicians and the people of Delhi at large, as a necessity, they have to be convinced, as to what planning can produce in terms of community benefits. At present Delhiites are disillusioned with master plans and planning.

The task of today's urban planners in Delhi calls for a knowledge of the process and causes of capital's urban growth, which has been phenomenal, as well as those of Delhi's economy and its social structure. Economic factors have been ignored in the urban planning process, although they are very much responsible to a large extent for Delhi's growth.

Urban planning in Delhi must aim at devising ways and means to increase economic productivity of the population, especially the urban poor, and improve urban efficiency by eliminating bottlenecks and breakdowns in the delivery of various urban services, such as water supply, power, mass transportation and the like, which impose costs on workers, businesses and consumers.

Urban planning in Delhi must move away from the present emphasis solely on land use planning, to guiding the very complex, interrelated process of social, economic and physical change, that is so evident in Delhi.

The planning Administration in Delhi has to broaden its field of interest and operation so as to include the entire complex of inter-related urban problems, physical, social and economic. In fact the city or town planning profession in the country needs to reassess its position, reassess its practice, theory and research to enable it to provide answers to growing number of problems confronting, not only Delhi, but also other cities in India.

The Town Planning profession must come face to face with the changing needs of Delhi's population. There is, thus, a need to redefine urban planning in the context of contemporary problems and situations. This, probably, is one of the most urgent matters which planners must address–it brooks no delay. Ever since the introduction of urban planning in India, over four decades ago, there has been no review of the urban planning system in operation to evaluate its effectiveness. As a result, there have been no reforms introduced to ensure that there is no gap between contemporary urban planning theory and practice on the one hand, and the capacity of the planning machinery to perform the functions for which it was set up on the other. This is a wake up call for the Institute of Town Planners, India, and all the institutions that train urban planners in the country, to review planning system in operation, as well as the current Town Planning Acts.

Actually, the DDA does not play any role, whatsoever in the implementation of the Master Plan, through the development projects of various agencies in Delhi. All that DDA contributes in the implementation process is of exercising zoning and development control measures. And instead of being a planning and policy making body and coordinator of implementation process, DDA is involved in development activities itself, which has progressively led to the marginalisation of urban planning activity, which is its legitimate function mandated by the Act.

The viability of the Delhi Master Plan depended on its being translated into a programme. Hence, the DDA should have formulated quinquennial capital urban improvement programmes, with a corresponding capital budget for Delhi's improvement and expansion, indicating the phases of the programmes, and their financing as well as indicating, the agencies responsible for their execution.

A viable plan is a programme. Therefore, DDA needed to prepare, on the basis of priorities, and resources, periodical plans–Five-Year Plans, for the physical improvement and development of Delhi, as was indicated in the Master Plan, 1981, and recommended by other public agencies operating in the Capital.

Various public improvements like urban-highways, street-widening, and other major public works could be incorporated in the preparation of urban development programme. Planning the improvements on a periodic basis, some of the major proposals in the public sector of the Master Plan could be implemented. Moreover, the improvement programme helps towards coordination of many urban development projects undertaken by various public agencies and would thus fit in the framework of the Plan. The vesting of capital budgeting function with DDA is the only dependable method of ensuring coordination among various agencies in Delhi and thereby achieving targets and goals of the Master Plan.

Concept of the Plan

Citizens of Delhi have very high expectations of what urban development plans can accomplish, and perhaps very vague notions of what a plan is or how it actually works.

Land is the basic resource of any city, in fact land is a national asset, and urban planning concerns itself with the controlled use of land, to the highest advantage, and for the general welfare of the people. Once land has been committed to a certain use it is difficult to change that use easily, so the planning process is of evaluating the advantages and disadvantages of one use as against another, and with the provision of adequate land for the various types of uses in a city. Land use planning and regulations are necessary to protect the public health, safety and general welfare of Delhiites. Zoning is used for regulating the use of land–the physical separation of potentially incompatible land uses. Zoning regulates the use of land and structures. The dimensional characteristics of permitted uses, such as minimum plot sizes, the placement of structures on plots that is minimum setbacks from property lines, the density of development, and the maximum heights of buildings, floor area ratio (building bulk).

In addition, zoning ordinances regulate landscaping, architectural design and features, signage, traffic circulation, and storm-water management. The general disposition of land uses, is an essential step toward a more definite regulation of the intensity, to which the land may be developed, and a limitation of the number of persons who are to be accommodated in commercial or residential areas.

Determination of the intensity of land use and the density of occupancy in all the use areas, by means of a comprehensive system of zoning and sub-division regulation. Control of land sub-division, especially for residential development is a basic method for directing the future growth of the city by exercising such a control. This step is not only important, as a means of encouraging an orderly and equitable utilization of the available land, but as the basis for control of the volume of traffic and the development of adequate road and parking facilities.

Planning for the development of the city begins with research and with the compilation of data relating to the physical, social, economic, cultural and political trends in the city. These generally include facts about the history, geography, geology, and natural resources, topography, weather, and prevailing winds in the city and its region ; about the population characteristics, employment and income levels ; about the land, the location, types and extent of residential, commercial and industrial areas, farms and open spaces ; about the economic base, industry, agriculture, trade and tax base ; about the transportation, streets, highways, parking places, and mass transit ; about public facilities, school, recreational areas and utilities and services.

Planners have to determine the reasons for the growth of Delhi. Identify the major activity that has accounted for the growth, in the past, and what is the likely trend of the future. Answers to these questions must be sought before any planning programme gets underway.

Urban planning oriented towards physical planning must operate in a matrix of social and economic factors. The Plan must be based on an understanding of the socio-economic needs of the Government of NCT of Delhi in which the Delhi metropolis is situated. Studies of the economic base of the metropolis, its soundness, deficiencies, and its prospects, have been completely overlooked.

DDA's urban planning has been narrowly restricted to elements of the physical pattern of the metropolis, without taking into consideration the social and economic aspects. The criteria of urban planning are social and economic as well as engineering. Therefore, physical plan must be based upon an understanding of the social and economic needs of Delhi. It must be recognised that physical solutions by themselves will not solve social and economic problems, but neither can economic vitality, community stability and environmental health be sustained without a coherent and supportive physical framework.

There are different ways in which plans for urban development work : They include agendas and policies, as means of framing the actions, implied by the plan. The vision, design and strategy aspects of the Plan, are most pertinent to figuring out the substantive logic of a plan, and thus precede these agendas and policies. Agenda is a list of things to do, and identifies issues or action to be undertaken by different agencies in the metropolis. Policy simplifies decision making. There is no adhocism in decision making. Decisions are guided by policies made.

Vision is an image of what Delhi could be ; it is a graphic and verbal description of future livable Delhi, what Delhi would look like after proposed changes occur.

Decline of Urban Planning

Nationwide, the urban development authorities do planning anyway they like. In most cities planning has completely disappeared. In Delhi, they haven't planned for years.

Urban planning in Delhi has suffered a precipitous decline. How and why did vital urban planning go into eclipse? Every profession needs to have faith in its ability to produce the results it desires. Urban planners in DDA lost that faith. Instead have become application-acceptors and permit-dispensers. They are not planners in the traditional sense of the word–individuals who give physical shape to the future. Delhi Development Authority surrendered responsibility to others, principally developers and builders, who have become increasingly free to subdivide land and build as they choose.

It's urban planning without any direction. The urban planning system that was initiated in the early 1960s in the capital has collapsed. The hopes and aspirations of the Delhiites aroused by the creation of DDA, and the initiation of planned development process, have been frustrated and eroded the credibility of urban planning. Today people in Delhi live in much more inhospitable urban environment than they did before the DDA. The prolonged exercise to decongest Delhi and check the flow of migrants to Delhi in search of employment has virtually proved a non-starter. Adhocism, expediency and political considerations figure more in decision making, thereby compromising what is necessary and good for Delhi.

Traditional approaches to urban (city) planning set out to document a finite long-term master plan that once legally adopted, formed the basis for infrastructure and services investment and a detailed system of land use regulations and development controls.

This form of urban planning worked well in countries with urban conditions characterised by slow growth, high average incomes, effective land use regulations and enforcement procedures, and also in the many developing countries including India, to which it was exported.

Experience has shown, that traditional approaches to urban planning have been found wanting, although they continue to be used in India in general and in Delhi in particular. This is so because of insufficient concern with financial implications of the plan proposals; lack of coordination with sectoral socio-economic, and financial strategies for urban development in which the master plan is seen as an end in itself rather than one component in the management of Delhi urban area ; uncertainty about the relationship between spatial and economic planning ; too rigid to keep abreast with the demands of increasingly rapid urbanisation ; the people of Delhi and their community organisation are not meaningfully involved in the planning process.

Urban planning has not taken roots not only in Delhi but in the rest of the country. Neither the politicians nor the bureaucracy gives any importance to planned urban development. One of the deficiencies of national economic development planning was that it ignored or overlooked local urban planning as an integral part of the national planning process.

Urban planning failed in Delhi because it is impossible to solve present and future problems of the city with yesterdays concepts. And also because of the neglect in considering urban planning as a part of democratically elected Municipal Government.

The urban planning process can no longer be regarded, solely in terms of preparing a master-plan for the physical features of the city. Planning limited only to this aspect of city life, is no longer adequate, because the field of the city government activity has expanded. The planning of today and of the immediate future must, if it is to survive as a distinct function of governance, be adjusted to the changes we see in urban life and government. To plan the future of the national capital without including, as a vital consideration, such matters as the condition of the local economic structure and its relation to the state and national structure, proliferating traffic, public transportation and deteriorating environment, which are central problems in urban life of Delhi. Then planning cannot be truly comprehensive if it treats them lightly or not at all.

There is a need for an urban development strategy for the national capital aimed at achieving balanced economic growth, social progress, and people-friendly environment; partnership among all developmental players in the capital; and resource mobilisation, public and private, financial as well as non-financial.

An important element in the weakness of urban planning body–DDA lay in the fact that it consisted mostly of persons who had peripheral knowledge of urban planning. DDA lacks the knowledge and resources to find solutions to various urban problems it is confronted with, and the inability to grasp the underlying conditions and to foresee their changes, or adequately influence them, or the absence of a mechanism to observe and take change into account as time passed. Most members of DDA are amateurs insofar as experience in urban planning and urban governance is concerned. Secondly, DDA's failure to build up experienced planning staff because of promotion on the basis of seniority, rather than capability. Urban planning is one of the applied sciences, the province of specially trained professionals. To make urban planning more responsive to the changing needs of rapidly growing Delhi, the Act has to be reviewed and revised. The present form of urban planning and the institution established for the purpose under the DDA Act has been ineffective.

The Urban Challenge

The complex problems of Delhi have aroused public sentiments, making it necessary for the powers-that-be to turn their attention to improving the quality of life for all in the metropolis. The urgency for solutions to the problems of Urban Delhi has increased. The issues that must be grappled with, have not only increased in number, but they have also become more complex.

It is quite obvious, that the problems of the spread out metropolis of Delhi are gigantic. It is also quite obvious, that these problems cannot be left to the hazard of solving themselves. For, it is true, that the future of Delhi, will be the result of the conglomeration of innumerable individual decisions of the people, it is also true, that trends can be directed towards a common good or can be left to entangle common good or can be left to entangle themselves in innumerable conflicts.

The free and easy meeting of problems as they arise will no longer suffice. We must look for solution of current problems in terms of the predictable future. Laissez-faire approach to urban development leads to repeating the mistakes of the past, which stood in the way of change.

"Cities are not organisms. They do not grow or change of themselves or reproduce or repair themselves". "It is human purpose and human willfulness that drives the making of cities." states Kevin Lynch and as Barbara Ward put it: "Neither in developed countries of the West, nor in the developing ones in the East, do good cities just grow in this age, they have to be guided and corrected."

Urban planning has a great deal to offer, in providing a means for evaluating the problems and pointing out the direction for sound growth and development. Urban planning has a full vision for the future, whereas the other departments of city government or public agencies or organisation in Delhi myopically concentrate on their individual problems and projects. Urban planning offers the most logical approach to solving city's problems arising from rapid growth and expansion, as well as from changing conditions affecting the inner city. Through proper urban planning, Delhi can be made both efficient and attractive. Well planned city is the symbol of pride and prestige of a nation–especially when that city is Delhi, the nation's capital. It is also indicative of people's or society's planned and systematic approach to life itself.

A New Paradigm in Urban Planning

To continue with the current approach to urban planning, at the scale of present metropolitan Delhi, with its complexity and dimensions of the contemporary urban problems is an anachronism. We need to radically revise our concept of urban planning.

In today's context urban planning in Delhi must be seen as a dynamic, adaptive, iterative and continuous process of anticipating, planning and managing social and economic change, brought about by free market reforms and globalisation.

There is need to device and adopt a new paradigm in urban planning, that provides a framework within which all public agencies and departments in Delhi can operate and which embodies programmes of action which are realistic in terms of resource availability. Urban planning currently being practiced, must shift from the focus on the statutory power of long-range vision of the metropolis, to the short-term management of the urban system. Urban system concists of five elements–Nature: Physical environment, land, water, air, flora and fauna; Man: the individual; Society: The social system; Shells: Buildings; Networks: Roads, transportation, water, power, telecommunication. We need to device a planning system based on a two-fold strategy: one concerned with policy planning. Policy planning focuses on performance goals for metropolitan Delhi as a whole in a long-term horizon. The other with programme planning, which focuses on achievement of goals for specific functional activity or sector or the subject area, that is of concern to the metropolis for short-term and medium-range projects.

Policy plan is formulated for the entire metropolis, whereas programme planning is done through the preparation of quinquennial and annual 'ACTION PLAN'. The Policy Plan is not a rigid design for the future, but a flexible framework in which both public and private action can achieve common objectives and policies. Being a policy plan, it has to be formulated in the context of national and state or regional planning policies.

For coordinating development programmes, among the sectors and across geographic space, quinquennial Plan is prepared as an urban development programmes for a period of five years, with a corresponding capital investment plan, which also identifies the agencies responsible for implementing the programmes. It indicates notional location of projects to be implemented, and provide guidelines for preparing detailed project plans. It lays down planning standards and urban design criteria conducive to local needs.

The planning and programming of all urban development activities covering the entire metropolis, as distinct from only a few development projects, enables the translation of the Policy Plan into metropolitan wide programme planning, corresponding to the national and State Five-Year Plans of economic development, and thus forming a capital investment plan as a budgetary tool, and also as an instrument for coordination and execution of public and private sector projects, in additional to inter-governmental coordination.

The final stage of the urban planning process is the Action Plan, a device for detailed planning and design, and implementation of programmes and projects for specific areas within the framework of the quinquennial Plan, be they redevelopment or new development. The Action Plan provides the flexibility for accommodating short-term changes in the overall Policy Plan. It is an application of the Policy Plan strategy, a basis for coordinating public and private development and a device for getting local and detailed planning issues before the concerned authorities in the metropolis. It provides guidelines for preparing detailed layout plans or site plans by both public and private agencies in Delhi.

Urban development plan for the National Capital can only be realised if day-to-day decisions are influenced by the plan, and if each operating agency is guided by considerations of overall planning for Delhi. The government of National Capital Territory of Delhi pays little or no attention to urban problems, despite having powers to regulate the metropolis. The government of NCT of Delhi must shift policy from completely unfettered laissez-faire approach, to one devised to urban growth management strategy, for improved planning and development process, both at NCT and urban level. By bringing the diverse pieces of planning, going on in the metropolis of Delhi, by various agencies, departments, into integral whole, from which planning needs may be derived.

Design strategic 'plan' for the national capital, in which the roles and objectives of different agencies and sectors are specified. To show the relationships between parts, to adjust the individual parts, to bring together agencies which are involved in conflict, or which need coordination, to try to reconcile differences, and to summarise the current status of existing plans. Achieve a high degree of integration and coordination through a planning mechanism. Identify different agencies in the capital involved with urban development–DTC, Electricity, Water-Sewerage, roads, traffic.

Urban planning for the National Capital must involve partnerships among private sector entrepreneurs, non-governmental organisations, residents welfare associations and individuals who are interested in making Delhi a better place.

Because of governmental fragmentation which exists in the metropolis of Delhi, coordination of action for implementation of the Plan is imperative. This coordination would be greatly facilitated through the existence of a single authority encompassing the entire metropolis with clearly defined powers of coordination.

Management Techniques

Urban planning is central to growth management process in Delhi. Urban planning is a comprehensive, coordinated and continuing process, the purpose of which is to help Delhi's public and private decision makers arrive at decisions which promote the common good of society. The process includes:

Identification of Delhi's problems or issues;

Research and analysing to provide definitive understanding of such problems or issues; Setting of goals and objectives, to be attained in alleviating problems or resolving issues; Development and evaluation of alternative methods to attain agreed upon goals and objectives; Recommendation of appropriate course of action from among the alternatives; Assistance in implementation of approved plans and programmes; Evaluation of action taken to implement approved plans and programmes in terms of progress towards agreed upon goals and objectives; and a continuing process of adjusting plans and programmes in light of the results of such evaluation or to take into account changed circumstances.

The policy plan/master plan is a product of this planning process. A policy plan is not static, but must be updated regularly in response to the effect of growth management strategies and changing conditions in Delhi.

- The policy plan should embody a vision of what Delhi wants to become and how it intends to get there. This vision should serve as an overall policy guide for public and private decisions that affect urban development, including the implementation of land use regulations and other growth management strategies.

There is a general prejudice against urban planning as a curtailment of freedom to develop and build as they chose. For the vested interest, urban planning is an obstacle in the laissez-faire competitive market. There is tendency to eschew urban planning. The authorities at local level presume that they can easily and quickly assess the reality of a situation and then with equal speed and lack of error, know what to do. In today's complex urban settlement like metropolitan Delhi, and particularly in situations that are maddeningly novel, it is not a good strategy.

Politicians and bureaucrats, see urban planning as something outside the sphere of day-to-day administration. Their lack of understanding to appreciate the need for urban planning, may be attributed in large measure, to the narrow concepts of urban planning, thus far portrayed by the city planners themselves. Urban planning is seldom presented as extending beyond physical improvement programme.

Lack of imagination and courage to envision the changes of our times call for, the planners are always wary about the obstacles they will face in the way of change. I hope these younger generation of timid planners take a less respectful attitude towards established values and have the imaginative and courageous outlook our changing times demand.

Planning profession must be repaired, planners need to be educated in the importance of the physical settings they are shaping. They need to acquire the skills they have neglected for years. These skills must be linked to a compelling purpose and vision, something that planning has sorely lacked. As planners become more capable, it will be incumbent on the public and especially on businesses to treat planners with greater respect than has been the norm. A new appreciation of planners, as people, who think might begin to dispel the apprehensive atmosphere that has made planning an unappealing line of work for the bright and dynamic.

Urban Renewal

Successful cities are not static. A place cannot be frozen in time. Thus, as Delhi continues to evolve, so too, should our efforts to ensure its success. Similarly, observations on what ingredients make for successful cities, continually change in response to changing needs, opportunities and circumstances.

Indeed, successful cities constantly experiment with a broad array of growth management techniques, to retain distinctiveness and protect key natural and cultural assets. By focusing on key assets and by building strong consensus for protection and sensitive development, successful city can be created and sustained.

Urban planning in Delhi has been focused mainly on guiding expansion to the metropolis, and not with correcting the consequences of the past growth. The problem of urban planning is not only primarily one of guiding city growth, it is a matter also of replanning areas already built. The older parts of Delhi metropolis, forming the urban core, and which are the nucleus of the metropolis, have reached their level of physical obsolescence and functional inefficiency, are in need of rebuilding to adept them to the present day needs of the capital.

Rebuilding of the older parts of Delhi, is a process that has been going on as long as they have existed. But this rebuilding is undertaken on a piecemeal and haphazard manner. As a consequence, old communities are eradicated and local identity destroyed. Historically, the older parts, what constitutes the "Inner city" has been the centre of the Delhi metropolis and has certain advantages, because its location is good, because city growth followed important transportation routes and the site per se had other material relationship with its surroundings.

But how does a metropolis like Delhi change its ways and take a new lease of life? It does so through the process of urban renewal, which demonstrates how an old city can be revitalised through integrated planning and massive civic effort.

Urban renewal is a powerful tool for improving the physical quality, functional and, economic efficiency of the metropolis as a whole. However, urban renewal has to be planned and programmed, as an integral part of a full-scale programme of the overall plan of the National Capital. Cooperation of private and public action is *sine quo non* for a successful urban renewal programme, because neither private nor government can do the whole job separately.

In Old Delhi, for instance, the building plots are too small, and often irregular in shape. Comprehensive renewal makes it necessary to reconstitute the plots for rebuilding. Besides, the streets are narrow and utilities and services inadequate. Such a situation is not simply conducive for private builders, who only deal with building site or plot. They cannot solve the greater "area problem", hence there is little opportunity for successful comprehensive urban renewal, solely on a private basis. Private enterprise require city government's participation and support, through public assembly of land, by means of 'town planning schemes' and other public measures, for creating desirable new land uses in a redesigned urban pattern. On the other hand, city government needs private builders to develop plots or sites made available, so as to create new social and economic values, which is the ultimate goal of urban renewal.

Radical urban renewal has not been introduced. Urban repair, that is piecemeal changes to the extant fabric, was the customary procedure. Fighting Municipal Government, which loves the quick fix, the instant "urban renewal" development which is often too big, too sudden, and anti-urban.

Urban Renewal is a comprehensive process of reorganisation and rebuilding of rundown areas of Delhi– revitalisation of deteriorated areas of the metropolis.

The delays, the mistakes, and the contradictions, and shortcomings of the past and present should not obscure the fact that Delhi metropolis can be transformed in the direction, and to the extent we desire. However, to effect the transformation it is essential first to have a clear sense of direction and objective and then to have the will to act.

It is also necessary to understand the forces that have shaped the metropolis. Only then can we have confidence in our ability to design and institute methods for effecting change that will produce satisfactory results.

A city is always in transition. It can never be completed and because of this there can be no final, once-and-for-all solution to the city's problems. The goal is always advancing, constantly shifting and altering, and usually enlarging. Changing ideas and changing needs dictate corresponding changes in the urban form. While change is always taking place, it does not take place in all parts of the city at the same time and in equal degree. Each generation inherits the city from the previous one, adds to it, uses what has been inherited or newly built until that has passed the margin of utility, and then replaces the outworn parts of the city. For a city to remain dynamic, renewal, like inheritance must be a continuous process.

This underscores the need for cooperative effort between MCD, Government of NCT of Delhi and private enterprise. Government alone can do slum clearance under appropriate laws. The private builders are already doing the job of rebuilding by buying plots or existing buildings, and rebuild high value structures, and sell at a profit. Therefore, the government should go for comprehensive urban renewal, whereby the city reaps the benefits. Planning and designing a new city according to some ideal is easy, but it takes real creativity to rebuild an existing and functioning city that just needs maintenance and strengthening.

The rebuilding of down town Connaught Place is not enough; a city deserted at night by its leading citizens is only half a city. If it is to continue as the dominant cultural force in Delhi's life the city must have a core of people to support its theaters, museums, its shops and its restaurants. For it is the people who like living in the city who make it an attraction to the visitors who don't. It is the city dwellers who supports its style, without them there is nothing to come down town to. One hears so much about how government is to blame for everything, that the best way to achieve development of the right kind is to encourage the private sector to do it. In many cases this is true, although not automatically. Citizen initiative and citizen control with appropriate, but modest government support. A strong local leader is a must.

The key to genuine revitalisation and economic development is a process, not product; incremental change, not instant transformation, modest local private investments, not massive infusion of Government revenues. Rejuvenate neighbourhoods, central business areas, District Centres (Nehru Place etc.) to preserve and enhance the qualities that would make Delhi so appealing.

Urban Villages

Unbriddled urbanisation in Delhi, has in its wake engulfed number of rural villages that have been there for centuries. In the process, these villages have become an integral part of the Delhi urban area. The livelihood of the inhabitants of these villages is no longer agriculture. Notwithstanding, the villages have been isolated from the urban planning process. There is no policy on urban villages in the successive Master Plans for Delhi. The local government has laid down a separate set of building regulations for urban villages quite different from the once prescribed for the urban area of Delhi, with disasterous consequences.

Because of the pressure on urban land, the urban village settlements are being rebuilt to a higher density on piecemeal basis. The high density building development is superimposed on the rural pattern of streets and land subdivision. The building activity in the urban villages is predominantly confined to commercial use, which attracts and generates high volume of vehicular traffic. It is ironical that on the one hand high intensity commercial building are permitted to come up, and on the other the capacity of the abutting streets is not increased to cater to the volume of traffic nor is there provision for parking of vehicles.

Rebuilding of the urban villages, without a comprehensive redevelopment has created environmental problems within the villages which have impacted on the surrounding urban areas. To cite a few examples of rebuilt villages like Shahpur Jat, Begumpur, Kalu Sarai area standing testimony to unplanned rebuilding of villages in Delhi.

While preparing the first Master Plan for Delhi, 1962 in the late 1950s, the Town Planning Organisation had prepared a prototype redevelopment plan for the village of Kotla Mubarakpur, knowing fully well that urbanisation would create a demand for rebuilding of the urban villages.

The redevelopment plan for Kotla Mubarakpur provided a framework within which the rebuilding could be done and of integrating the redevelopment village with the urban area of Delhi.

It is unfortunate that the Plan for Kotla Mubarakpur never got translated into action, instead it must be collecting dust on the shelves of Town and Country Planning Organisation.

Planning as a Function of Urban Government

After independence city planning got detached from problems of administration, yet despite this fact, planning in the long run has tended to reflect the expanding scope of municipal government in India.

In order to keep urban planning from urban politics or urban political influence, the setting up of independent urban development authorities in metro-cities outside the governmental structure was justified by the bureaucracy. Today many of these urban development authorities are inactive. They continue their interest to exercising development controls and public works. The autonomy and the amateur character of these development authorities militates against the best interest of city planning. These authorities in reality have fallen far short of their potential usefulness. DDA a separate urban planning agency, only tenuously connected with MCD. DDA has not been an effective instrument for serving the continuously changing needs of the Delhi metropolis.

The dynamism of urban planning and the effects of implementation of the several ingredients of the Delhi Plan underscores the desirability of integrating the planning process with that of implementation. This concept of a separate agency (DDA) that controls city government (MCD) as regards the ingredients of the Delhi Plan or of its implementation has not proved to be sound. Urban planning should spring from the people per se. If the responsibility is placed on the city government (MCD), it is probable that the plan that emerges will prove more acceptable and easier of implementation.

Under these circumstances, a re-examination of the structure and function of the present city government

(MCD) is necessary. The 74th Constitution Amendment Act laid emphasis on devolution of planning function to local bodies, and involvement of people in the planning and decision making processes. The first three items of Twelfth Schedule relate to: (i) urban planning including town planning, (ii) regulation of land use and construction of buildings, and (iii) planning for economic and social development. Besides, the Act provides for constitution of District Planning Committees (DPC) and Metropolitan Planning Committees (MPC) to prepare the draft development plans taking into consideration the Plans prepared by Panchayats and Municipalities.

We need an urban planning body at the Metropolitan Government level, with wide perspective, specialised urban planning skills, and adequate resources, to prepare an overall policy plan for guiding the development and redevelopment of the national capital, revising and adjusting where necessary each action agency's plans. This will require a close and continuous coordination of activities between the urban planning body and the various agencies.

Unless some rational and meaningful urban planning with centralised coordination is undertaken in Delhi, the urban revolution, the capital is faced with, may prove more hazardously polluting to Delhi's future potential than all its other problems combined. Urban planning process is an aspect of the process of metropolitan government. It is government looking to the future, determining desirable objectives and seeking the best and most economical means for achieving them.

The main reason for the failure of planning lies in not making planning as a part of the administration of local urban government, where it would have been closer to the city council, the Commissioner and Mayor and other city Government departments. Instead an independent body, the DDA was set up in place of the Delhi Improvement Trust. Planning no matter how good, is useless unless it influences official action. As long as the planning agency (DDA) is outside the city governmental structure, it will tend to encounter resistance from public officials as an invasion of their responsibility and jurisdiction. Planning is essential to good government. Planning will never rise above its present status until it is made an essential part of the local government.

5

Regional Approach to Urban Development

In the course of the Central Economic Planning process in India, investments have gone wherever the conditions were conducive for investments, which has led to metropolitan concentration and greater regional imbalances. Infrastructure has to be built up in other areas of the country to create conditions for even distribution of economic activities and balanced growth.

The unabated growth and concentration of population and economic activities in the Delhi metropolis, has led to acute exploitationary conditions, not only within its confines, in terms of access to land, economic opportunities and income distribution, but also in wider sense, in thwarting the growth of ring towns in the National Capital Region (NCR).

We need to deal with the problems of urban deterioration in more positive way. Not by congesting Delhi's urban core further or by building new housing on its suburban fringes, instead by developing the so-called ring-towns in the National Capital Region.

The powers that be in Delhi feel that, we will make our mess now and clean it up later, when we can afford it. But as Delhi demonstrates, when a city grows as fast and in an unbridled a fashion as Delhi has, there may be no later. Let it be clearly understood what the City Government in Delhi does or does not, to correct past mistakes and deal with anticipated future development, is of vital concern to everyone living in the national capital; this includes business and industry as well. It has a direct bearing on stability of investments, on the ability to do business and on the amenities of home and family life for the millions of Delhi's inhabitants. For thousands of years Delhi's fabric has been built, knocked down, rebuilt and knocked down again. Delhi as we see today is a mess.

The Planning Team that prepared the Delhi Master Plan in the early 1960s limited to Delhi urban area, had the foresight to draw the attention of the government, of not merely confining planned development to Delhi urban area, but on a much larger scale. Because, it was realised that unless one plans on a regional scale, any immediate action remedies for Delhi would inevitably fail. For even if large amount of housing was planned and built, and even if water, power and sewerage system was made available, Delhi would have failed to catch up. Because the major problem of Delhi, was massive migration from rural areas and smaller towns. Nearly 50 per cent of Delhi's urban growth is contributed by migration.

Therefore, it was necessary to equally plan the region of the national capital, so that smaller towns around it offered employment opportunities and reasonable living conditions, to share the burden of rapidly increasing urban population. Why create new towns, when existing towns are under-utilised. The objectives of economic efficiency and social justice suggest that growth be focussed in towns that are already, atleast partially developed.

The notion of relieving congestion of big cities by building new towns is not a recent one. Between 300 B.C. and 150 A.D. Romans built cities, either where no city previously existed or where a small village stood. The maximum population and size were determined before construction began. The planners then allotted adequate space for houses, shops, squares, and temples. They determined how much water would be needed and the number and size of streets, sidewalks, and sewers. By planning this way they tried to satisfy the needs of every individual–rich and poor alike.

The planners agreed that when a city reached its maximum population a new city should be built elsewhere. They recognised the danger of over population. A city forced to grow beyond its walls not only burdened the existing water, sewage, and traffic systems but eventually destroyed the farmland on whose crops the people depended.

No matter what brought about their creation, the cities were designed and built to serve the needs of all the people who lived within them. This kind of planning is the basis of any truly successful city. The need for it today is greater than ever.

First the surveyors selected the place where the city would be built. They chose a flat but sloping site, to ensure proper drainage, that was high enough to avoid future floods.

In the master plan for the city, the entire area was divided by roads into a chessboard pattern. Almost all of the blocks were eighty yards square. A high wall was designed around the city in which fortified gates were located where the main streets cut through. Around the city, but inside the wall a thirty–foot–wide strip of land was marked off, representing the sacred boundary of the city within which the land was protected by the gods.

The city planners indicated those facilities which served all the residents. While the master plan allowed much freedom for the residents to determine the appearance and character of the city, through the buildings they would construct for themselves, it decreed that no privately owned building could be higher than twice the width of the street on which it abutted. This was to ensure that sunlight always reached the streets. The plan also required all persons whose buildings faced one of the main streets to build, at their own expense, shelter over the sidewalk for the comfort and protection of all pedestrians.

More than five hundred years ago, Leonardo da Vinci proposed to the Duke of Milan, that he build ten cities, each of thirty thousand population, to ease the overcrowding of Milan. However, the concept of the modern new town is distinctly British invention. Ebenezer Howard, a Londoner, was the first person to apply political intelligence to the problem of the overgrowth and congestion of cities. He sought to replace the planless over expansion of the big city with a planned "colonisation" to draw off the surplus population. To achieve this, he proposed to build largely self-sufficient communities, limited in size and density of population, but big enough to sustain a variety of industries and to satisfy the everyday wants of the population. Howard called this new urban form the "Garden City".

In his book 'Garden Cities of Tomorrow', Ebenezer Howard, proposed to test the possibility of creating a viable urban form, by building an experimental model, that would set a new pattern, for the future city development. Instead of urban agglomeration, planned dispersal, instead of concentration, decentralisation, instead of disorganisation a higher type of unity.

There are also more immediately tangible and visible reasons for tackling the capital region. The motorised transportation has erased the administrative boundaries of Delhi and the cities/towns in the region. Development controls imposed in Delhi have simply led to haphazard development just across the Delhi State border, as evident from the urban development activities in the bordering State of Uttar Pradesh and Haryana. Therefore, the problems shared by Delhi and its immediate hinterland is a mutual one, not merely Delhi's concern.

The National Planning Commission had indicated in its fourth Five-Year Plan, that it was necessary to create larger planning regions and to provide by law, that the plans formulated by the regional planning authority are implemented by the local city governments. Planning to be effective requires legal structure for formulating and implementing the plans. Both the rapidity of the population growth in the National Capital Region and the urgency of the problems related thereto, led the town and country planning organisation of the Government of India to prepare the NCR planin the early seventies. The Plan, then, was designed to serve in an advisory capacity to the constituent states and local governments in the region for whom it provided a ten-year perspective on the development of the National Capital Region.

The Plan's objective was that of maximising growth by a planned development of NCR and to mould and refashion the region, both physically and economically.

The goals for the planning of NCR were stated as follows—(i) Well organised urban places in the NCR in physically efficient pattern and socially desirable environment with effective participation of the local bodies, that will sustain dynamic growth in keeping with natural goals; (ii) rational and orderly growth of Delhi as the National Capital, symbolising the life and aspirations of the nation; (iii) integrated and coordinated development of the transportation system, sources of water supply, flood control measures, drainage, and power supply; (iv) sustained development planning of the Region and effective implementation of the plan in close integration with the economic development of the nation.

The spur driving the TCPO to formulate the NCR plan was the concern, that if regional growth were uncontrolled, Delhi might possibly become a city of 10 million people of the year 2000, such growth obviously being at the expense of the nearby regional towns, and violating the holding capacity of Delhi, which was estimated atabout 5.3 million people. Today the population of Delhi has reached to more than 14 million.

The plan called for a national spatial development strategy to be put into effect, including the decentralisation of economic activity to curb the rural exodus, and to facilitate this the linkages between metropolitan cities, medium-sised towns, and the rural hinterland had to be effective.

The strategy adopted was to keep within manageable limits, both the population and area of urban Delhi. It was, therefore, recommended that Delhi be maintained as far as possible, as a compact-urban structure, with a possible population of 5.3 million by 1981. This involved diverting population concentration to 17 regional towns in Uttar Pradesh, Haryana and Rajasthan. These towns were enviscovied as compact towns with medium densities, with relative self-containment, in matters of workplaces and residences, but having trade and commerce and socio-cultural relationship with the Delhi metropolis. Circumferential transport facilities to open up the entire region were recommended to encourage interaction amongst the towns and prevent a major transport bottle neck at Delhi.

Such a plan meant putting a curb on the concentration of jobs in Delhi. The Plan's industrial policy was to exclude large scale and heavy industries from Delhi, but instead encourage small scale industries.

Decentralisation of selective wholesale trade from Delhi, with some consideration of the fact that the trade transactions themselves might be continued in Delhi, but not the related goods handling, was recommended. Decentralisation of the Central Governments offices not required to be in Delhi was strongly recommended.

The NCR Plan called for coordinated and integrated development of regional utilities and services, including water, drainage and flood control, power and recreational and community facilities.

The regional land use policies incorporated in the National Capital Regional Plan, proposed optimisation of residential densities in Delhi. The plan also proposed for land being acquired and developed as well as the creation of a Statutory Regional Planning Board to prevent speculative and unauthorised subdivision of land and to regulate other development projects.

The criminal task was to make the Planning and Implementation Committee of the then Advisory High Power Board an effective instrument in coordinating the preparation of functional and detailed plans, in conformity with the regional plan, and their implementation. The Planning and Implementation Committee was also to make efforts to incorporate detailed plans in the Uttar Pradesh, Haryana and Rajasthan State Five-Year Plans and Annual Plans, to provide the necessary funds by treating the NCR as a "special area" requiring more than ordinary accommodation on the part of the Planning Commission, Ministries of the Central Government as well as the constituent state governments.

At that time serious difficulties were involved in carrying out the Plan's proposals. Because the then existing High Power Board was only Advisory, not in the NCR Plan. The High Powered Board in 1967 had urged that a statutory board be formed to give more power to implement the NCR Plan.

A special committee advised the Ministries of Urban Development Government of India to set up a statutory NCR Planning Board, which was formed years later and at present very much in existence.

The functions of the statutory board was of preparing regional plan for the national capital region; preparation of functional plans for different elements of the regional plan; preparation of sub-regional plans by the respective administrations of the Uttar Pradesh, Haryana and Rajasthan coordination of the implementation of regional, functional and sub-regional plans; and lastly review of the regional plans periodically to meet the changing needs of the settlements in the region. An establishment of a revolving fund to be made available to the NCR statutory board was proposed as a source of assistance to the state and local governments of the region for implementation of the plan.

Neither the DDA nor the NCR authority did make any headway in creating a balanced development of the national capital region. With the result Delhi has been swamped, and the most desperate attempts the authorities are making to cope with the problems of the capital, have fallen further and further behind.

Most new housing development is added on a piecemeal basis at the edge of present built-up areas. For the private builders this is the easiest and most "natural" location for the construction of middle-classes houses. However, if lacs of additional dwellings are added in this way, it creates an endless continuation of the urban sprawl, and greater distance between central areas of Delhi and the homes and since most white collar and professional jobs are concentrated in central areas, the journey-to-work is greatly extended.

With the emergence of NOIDA across the Yamuna River and of massive urban development in Gurgaon area in Haryana, one sees the evolution of a megalopolitan formation extending to the States of Uttar Pradesh and Haryana across the Delhi State border.

The massive urban development taking place in Gurgaon and Ghaziabad areas, are largely devoid of places worth caring about. They are soulless subdivisions, residential areas utterly lacking in community life. These residential areas should have been planned as neighbourhoods. Neighbourhood is an organic outgrowth of human needs–it is the traditional human habitat. Reconfiguration of 'placeless' sprawling exurbia into communities of real neighbourhoods, the conservation of natural environment and the preservation of our built legacy.

Haryana government has abrogated its responsibility for community making, to the private sector developers. The developer has been building whatever physical environment he wants at the public's expense. His approach to development of residential areas does not emanate from any physical vision. It has no images, no diagrams, no recommended models, only plots and streets. The developer has no clear picture of what he wants his residential area to be. His subdivision plan is not based on a specific vision of its physical form or of the kind of life that form would generate.

The suburban sprawl beyond the boundaries of Delhi State (Government of National Capital Territory) offers all the drawbacks and none of the advantages of either city or countryside. It nullifies the reduction of working hours by adding to the time required to travel between home and workplace. The suburban sprawl, a standard pattern of growth promoted by developers and builders, has produced insurmountable traffic problems and exacerbating social inequity and isolation–a traffic nightmare, everyone is forced to drive. Public transportation is rarely an option.

A need, therefore, exists for a planning process to start at a higher level which would lead to an overall development plan for the megalopolis within the NCR and to the necessary programme for alleviating the regional problems generated by urban development across Delhi border.

At present there is no authority to undertake such an effort, as the NCR Board is dysfunctional. If the growth of megalopolis is to be properly guided and its component parts provided with an overall coordinated plan for their functional participation within the broader system, the establishment of an appropriate institutional framework is of immediate importance. The lack of regional plan and programme for National Capital Region has impeded coordination between NOIDA, Haryana Urban Development Authority and the DDA.

Even since its inception, the National Capital Regional Planning Board has produced volumes of reports on regional development, which need to be translated into action on the ground. In order to develop ring towns located in the neighbouring States of Uttar Pradesh, Haryana, and Rajasthan, each State must set up Town Development Corporations under the umbrella of NCR Planning Board, for providing economic activities and job opportunities to the ring towns. The inordinate delay in developing ring towns has given rise to domitory towns across state border into Gurgaon in Haryana, with the concomitant problems of increasing traffic, into Delhi.

Capital's city government should recognise that the most meaningful urban planning occurs at the regional scale. Delhi's planning efforts are sabotaged by the actions of both UP and the Haryana Governments. When making local planning decisions, the city government must consider the impact of its initiatives on the entire region. Delhi does not have a governing authority of a scope appropriate to the metropolis. We need to have a metropolitan government with a man-made to handle transportation, environment, quality water, waste management, social services, affordable housing, economic development, higher education etc. must be addressed comprehensively.

The State Government is best able to promote regional planning, because the Central Government is distant, city government is myopic, and regional government is lacking. What is most needed at the Central Government level is a national policy on urban design.

6

Reinventing Urban Governance

The Municipal Corporation of Delhi (MCD) was constituted in the late 1950s. Prior to that the urban governance in Delhi was assigned to eight municipal and notified area committees, which formed greater Delhi, namely: Notified Area Committee (Civil Lines); Delhi Municipal Committee; Fort Notified Area Committee; New Delhi Municipal Committee; South Delhi Municipal Committee; Notified Area-Cantonment Board; West Delhi Municipal Committee; and Shahdara Municipal Committee. With the creation of MCD all these municipalities, with the exception of NDMC and the Cantonment Board, were abolished. The MCD has been functioning as a major City Government in the nation's capital for over five decades.

The present structure of urban government in Delhi–the MCD, goes back to the colonial period, designed to deal with predominantly a rural and agricultural society that India was then. The British created municipal governments, also known as local self-governments in cities for directly associating Indians with the administration of the country. As the Frenchman Alexis De Tocqueville wrote: "Grassroot democracy rests on the assumption that small political units, being close to the people, make possible the purest expression of self-government". Thus the city or town has often been considered the "natural home" of democracy. It is the place where the people exercise their power most directly and immediately. The basic problems of the people are local in character, and should be dealt with by local initiative. Municipal government serves also as the school for democracy, the most effective training ground for democracy lies in the field of local self-government. In fact, the creation of local self-government was perceived as the "cradle of democracy".

The Municipal Government structure we have inherited was never designed to cope with rapid urbanisation and its concomitant problems, that have overwhelmed Delhi. The municipal bodies then did not have to cope with the contemporary urbanisation and its concomitant problems faced with, or to manage a metropolis of Delhi of over 14 million inhabitants. We have inherited a framework of laws and procedures, wholly inappropriate to deal with the urban processes the nation's capital is confronted with. Notwithstanding, we have let this inherited structure continue, consequently MCD is unable to manage the problems generated by rapidly expanding Delhi metropolis and the economic change.

In order to make MCD the key agent of development, it needs enhanced political, institutional and financial capacity, perhaps access to more of the wealth generated in Delhi metropolis, so that MCD can adapt and deploy some of the vast array of tools available to address urban problems–tools such as the management of traffic and transportation in the capital. In fact it is the sheer mismanagement of the metropolis which is responsible for the mess we are in today. The MCD does not work efficiently, because it is so tangled in bureaucracy, that it is essentially dysfunctional. The bureaucracy is captive to a lot of silly rules and administrative procedures. We need a task oriented city government in the nation's Capital.

If this great metropolis of Delhi is to realise its full potential, it will be necessary to embark upon an intensive programme of political, administrative, technical and financial reforms at the Municipal Government level. Unfortunately, even after half century of independence, the inherited structure of Municipal Government remains unaltered, while its functioning has degenerated beyond measure. Today, political rather than civic considerations have dominated the area of Municipal Government in Delhi.

Inspite of the fact that more and more of the wealth and productivity of our country are being concentrated in the cities, the engines of economic growth, they are being grossly neglected by the State as well as the Central Government. The States fail to recognize, that it is in the larger aspects of urbanisation strategy, and in the development plans for specific cities, that social objectives of the society may best be reflected and furthered.

To successfully deal with problems that Delhi faces, we have to make local government more entrepreneurial, efficient, and performance driven. We have to discard the existing archaic bureaucratic model of city governance. The people of Delhi know that the present structure of Municipal Government has failed in building a better quality of life for them.

As reformers we cannot just limit our attack to the urban conditions we deplore in the metropolis. All of City Government in Delhi has to be changed. When Delhi was smaller city during the colonial period and right up to the time of independence, it was easily and efficiently governed. The challenges of today, however, has put pressure on the existing Municipal Government structure, that this structure could not handle.

With an unprecedented growth spurt for the metropolis of Delhi we must force the modernisation of the Municipal Government mired in the past. We need politicians with a focus on the future of Delhi—a visionary.

The Municipal Corporation of Delhi cannot continue in its present form, structure and thinking. Reforms in the basic character of governance are required. The MCD must be restructured and reoriented in its thinking to meet the needs of Delhi's population. We need to reform City Government by moving beyond traditional party politics, and solving problems pragmatically.

Urban Management

The management of urban development in Delhi is shared by Municipal Corporation of Delhi, New Delhi Municipal Committee, Rajdhani Power Company, The Delhi Development Authority and Public Works Department, all of whom function in an ad hoc and uncoordinated manner.

These multiplicity of agencies by the nature of their functions they perform, have virtually downsised the popularly elected municipal government in Delhi, with bureaucracy overwhelming the democratically elected City Council, but without any accountability. Bureaucratic growth, the mushrooming of city agencies was the response of the city to problems that had always existed, but were aggravated by the ever growing population of migrants.

Our political system has created a unique breed of legislators or councilors at City level, largely unqualified to legislate, who have sought election to feather their own nests, in order to wield or influence executive power. It has produced City Government in Delhi more skilled at politics than at policy or performance. It has distorted the voting preferences of Delhi's electorate that knows, which individual it wants, but not necessarily which policies. It has promoted corruption in public life.

Since local government is closer to the people, it should be more responsive to them. Therefore, the primary role of the mayor and municipal council should be leadership, reaching out beyond simply administering programmes and functions. They should mobilise the NGO and the private sector in public interest. This way local officials are personally responsible for the full range of local outcomes than would be the expected if they functioned only as administrators. Accountability is the key to better performance and resource mobilisation.

Good governance and effective performance requires public-interest oriented bodies out of local government, such as Resident Welfare Associations, special interest NGOs etc. working with local government and with each other. These community needs, apply pressure to see that they are addressed, and monitor the performance of the agencies that deal with them. Residents of neighbourhoods must realise that they cannot sit and wait for MCD to solve all of their problems.

Urban Planning as a Function of Local Government

Town planning was introduced in India in the early Twentieth Century by the British during the colonial rule. Town planning then was the legitimate administrative function of local government–the Municipal Government.

In Delhi, the creation of the Delhi Development Authority, in mid-1950s, for guiding the development of Delhi according to Plan, had urban planning detached from the functions of local government. The setting up of DDA as an independent autonomous urban development authority, outside the municipal government, was justified by the bureaucracy, for keeping urban planning from local politics and political influence.

The Delhi Development Authority working apart from the municipal governments in the capital, was another addition to the multiplicity of agencies operating in the Capital. Thus, the management of urban development activities was further fragmented. It happens that the autonomous DDA is only tenuously connected with MCD. This whole idea behind separating development functions from maintenance functions have eroded the relevance of the Municipal government to the extent of downsizing the democratic institution. The DDA is not answerable to the people of Delhi, who are expected to play a vital role in the planning and development of the city in which they live.

Experience has shown that DDA as an independent authority, under the administrative control of the Union Ministry for Urban Development, has not been really an effective instrument for serving the continuously changing needs of the national capital and its residents. It has not been responsive to Delhi's needs and conditions, as it is non-representative in character. It has not only weakened the Municipal Government by usurping its role, functionally and financially, but DDA itself has fallen far short of its potential usefulness.

Like so many other similar organisations in the country, DDA has virtually abandoned the original purpose for which it was created, and, instead has become more concerned about preserving itself, its prerogatives, its position and its power.

Experience has shown that the idea of a separate authority that will control municipal government as regards, either the desired ingredients of a plan or its execution does not appear to be sound. Planning for Delhi should spring from the people who live in Delhi. Therefore, placing responsibility of urban planning in the Municipal Government would ensure that the Plan for Delhi that emerges will prove more acceptable and easier of implementation. The Plan no matter how well conceived, is useless, unless it influences official action. Therefore, it requires the confidence and goodwill of those who decided public policy and that is the Municipal Council and not the DDA. As long as urban planning is kept outside Municipal Government, it will tend to encounter resistance from public officials, as invasion of their responsibility and jurisdiction. The bottom line is urban planning in Delhi will never rise above its present status until such time as it is made an essential part and function of city government.

The success of planning in city government is contingent upon good urban management. The success of management is contingent upon good planning. The official planning activities should be established firmly within the administrative hierarchy of municipal government.

Our system of urban governance has given control over the environment to thousands of speculators and builders, each seeking to increase his profits. Since the individual landowners and builders decisions are short-sighted and uncoordinated, they could result only in distructive disorder. Laissez-faire had thus created the metropolis of Delhi in its own image: Chaotic, ugly, and inhuman—a whole environment built by greed. What we need is a city government that would assert its mastery over self-seeking individuals—the landlords and builders.

Metropolitan Government

The Delhi Metropolis has reached unprecedented dimensions—a mega-city of over 14 million people. It has become too large and unwieldy to be governed as a single entity. The national capital is in need of a metropolitan government, based on federal principle. Metropolitan Delhi should have two tiers of government: one areawide to perform functions fitting into that classification, and another for local community to handle functions of a more parochial interest.

Water supply, drainage, both storm and sanitary, power supply, mass public transportation, law and order and urban planning should be areawide; while garbage collection, local street maintenance and parks and gardens would be appropriate for the lower tier government. Such a form of government is found in London and Toronto.

We need to put in place a metropolitan government to perform areawide functions, and township governments at the lower tier. Delhi metropolis should be divided into townships, with each township with a population of one million.

Township government is truest form of democracy, giving people the right to self-government. Allowing people to voice their opinions and know they are heard is critical to township government's survival or functioning effectively. It exists for the people and by the people. For it to be democracy for every Delhiites, he or she must be involved.

One does not have to become an elected official to the township council to become involved in township government. Township must have boards or committees comprising of local residents. Since townships offer a variety of municipal services, require many different individuals to sit on various boards and committees, like education, parks and recreation, water and drainage, power, urban planning and environmental protection. Delhiites must get involved in Township government and see how you can make a difference in the community/ neighbourhood in which you live.

As a mature democracy, the Metropolitan government for Delhi should have a Mayor-in-Council form of urban government, wherein, the administrative responsibility is concentrated in the hands of the Mayor, while policy making is a joint function of the Mayor and the Metropolitan Council. The Mayor is responsible for carrying out the established policy of the Metropolitan Government and for coordinating the efforts of the various metropolitan government departments. He is also responsible for the preparation of the annual budget, and for administering it once it is adopted by the metropolitan council. This allows for the whole financial picture and the needs of the various departments to be compared in financial policy making.

Mayor's control over administration gives constant oversight of the needs of the Delhi Metropolis as a whole and provides a vantage point from which to recommend policy. The Council in the Mayor-in-Council paradigm plays relatively subordinate role. It does not share in the performance of administrative duties. Its functions are limited to the exercise of legislative policy making and even this role is shared by the Mayor.

The Mayor appoints the city manager who functions as the supervisor of heads of various departments, prepares budget and personnel direction, coordination, provision of technical and professional advice to the Mayor.

The structure of the Metropolitan government for Delhi, like any other structures of government are tools. They are important, but like other machinery they may be modern or antiquated and are hence not all equally suited for present day governance. A tool will not operate itself, however, nor will the same one be equally effective in various kinds of cities. Local cultural circumstances will, no doubt, influence the type of structure that is needed and the quality of local government that will be produced from any chosen form.

Urban management has become more complex and challenging. National Capital has to develop new management tools to respond to new challenges. We must make urban governance more entrepreneurial, performance driven. While wealth is being created in the Metropolis, local government is unable or unwilling to access it sufficiently to address public needs. Since local government is supposed to be closer to people, it should be more responsive to them.

In this era of dramatic change, one of the biggest obstacles to our changing, is the machinery of government itself. Its been stuck in the past, wasting too much money, often ignoring the taxpayer, coping with outdated systems and archaic technology, and most of all, eroding the confidence of the people, that government can make change work for them.

Once in place, metropolitan government needs to provide order in the midst of urban chaos and anarchy. Delhiites are demanding a better quality of life, access to adequate clean water, waste disposal, drainage, sewage treatment, public education, adequate mass public transportation, electric power, traffic management, alongwith other urban services.

Managing the Delhi metropolis, through effective urban governance system, will be the key to long-term success and prosperity for all citizens of Delhi. While citizens must mobilise for the task of making Delhi a better place, it is Delhi's leaders of vision and courage and ability must lead the way.

Ultimately the successful implementation of greater participatory democracy requires a commitment from Delhi's political leadership, which must involve Delhiites in the formulation and implementation of policies and goals related to Delhi's environmental protection and conservation and urban development.

7

Voice of the People

The highest measure of democracy is neither the 'extent of freedom', nor the 'extent of equality', but rather the highest measure of participation.

—A.D. Benoist

We have an urban crisis in Delhi, of huge and growing proportions, that is already affecting the well-being of the inhabitants. While the nation's capital is faced with the crisis, there is no political will, no urban strategy, no priority and no direction in the systematic response to the crisis, from powers-that-be, whom destiny has saddled with authority. Some of the most glaring consequences of this benign neglect, and an absence of coherent urban development policy for the national capital, is reflected in the runaway urbanisation and the appalling living conditions.

Delhiites cannot wait until urban problems reach staggering proportions, before action is taken. They will have to assume more responsibility, for their own well-being and that of the urban community as a whole. The complex problems which have developed over the years should arouse public sentiments, making powers-that-be to turn their attention, to improving the quality of life for all the people in the nation's capital.

Are the Delhiites too involved with themselves to be bothered with public life? Are the young Delhiites passionate enough, about staking their claim to the future? There are scores of young people in Delhi, who are for saving the environment and protecting city's heritage. Why doesn't that activism translate into faith in the democratic process. Many perhaps feel that it does not matter, because only people with lot of money, political clout and power really have a say in what happens. The vast majority of the inhabitants of the Delhi metropolis ek out a mere existence. They have little feeling of having any stake in society or of their civic status, or of any hope that better days lie ahead. I don't believe that only extraordinary people change things, on the contrary, many significant social movements are the result of many ordinary, brave human beings choosing to take control of their lives.

However, young people do feel that the flaws of modern politics, particularly the influence of money and difficulty of obtaining objective information, push them to take refuge in ironic detachment. Political leadership in the nation's capital, should understand young people's non-participation as a strong message in itself. The system needs to be cleansed of special interest money and made more accessible to the grassroots of young India. While the flaws in the system are certainly to blame, our crisis of faith in self-government runs even deeper, exacerbated by the present day political culture.

Looking back half-century as an independent nation, and the earlier history of our struggle for self-governance, during the British Raj, it needs to be underscored, that democracy in India, despite the resilience it has shown, has yet to strike deep roots among the majority of Indians. As residents of Delhi, there is plenty we can do, should do, and must do, because our political system of representative democracy is based on the premise, that we the people, can govern ourselves and that, in fact, we should want to govern ourselves. That means we cannot leave it up to the politicians and bureaucrats alone, at the local government level or the State level, to make all the decisions and do all the governing.

Local government is the government closest to the people, to provide immediate urban services to people where they live. The Municipal Corporation of Delhi is closest to you. You must turn to your city government to handle problems closest to you. Everyone of us should have an interest in influencing the policy decision of the MCD and other local agencies, because MCD and other concerned agencies affect everyone of us. MCD as the city government tries to solve our everyday problems. People of Delhi should be in touch with their respective city councilors, the complaints can greatly influence government decisions. City government decisions can also be influenced by citizen interest groups, who pressure City Council and city government officials through organised campaigns. Delhiites have a greater chance to influence the Council, the Mayor, especially if they organise. When enough citizens express their views, Councilors will pay attention.

Society cannot effectively resolve conflict or competing demands and interests, generate new ideas, function democratically, or maintain stability unless individuals are free to express themselves. Without freedom of expression, the individual is not truly free and cannot be an active participants or maintain self-respect and dignity while functioning with others as part of society in Delhi. However, we as a people lack the effective means to be heard or to translate our wishes into reality through the political process. What is needed is a substantial expansion of the means accessible to ordinary people, for expressing their views effectively and for effective participation in the political process. If you want something, you have to make it happen.

A power influence on city government is the local media, electronic and the newspapers. People should use the media to express their opinions on civic affairs and on various problems they face and which affects their daily lives. The primary product of a newspaper is news. News is a unique, and uniquely important product. Presented at its best, news informs and enlightens the public of free societies like ours, and thereby safeguards and strengthens democracies. But presented dishonestly, unfairly or irresponsibly, as sometimes newspapers do, news can erode the public trust, on which the news media's own success depends; worse still corrode democratic systems of which it is so indispensably a part. For generations to come, democratization of information will be a powerful safeguard of representative government.

Maintenance of democracy requires an educated citizenry, knowledgeable about government. You, in Delhi, must get to know what the city government's responsibilities and obligations are, which they must fulfill. You must know what to demand. Empower Delhiites to become active participants in the city government process. The city government should be instituted for the common benefit, protection and security of the people in Delhi. We as people must demand transparency and accountability from our councilors in MCD and MLAs in the Delhi Assembly.

The government at the city level must be made less bureaucratic and more democratic. To have a functioning democracy we need to dismantle the stifling bureaucracy. We need a functioning democracy, which is about democratic disposition, habit and outlook. As citizens we must be habituated into democratic ideal and spirit. One of respect and responsibility, one in which large majority are capable of self-governance and prepared to display regard for others.

The ethos that guides our bureaucracy is against the spirit of age, which demands openness, transparency and public participation. Bureaucracy works in secrecy and discourages transparency and public participation in decision making. Excessive government and lack of public participation, destroys democracy, thwarts private initiative and smothers development. The 'glorified babu' is an anachronism in a democratic administration, a disincentive for growth and prosperity. The Indian Administrative Service (IAS) was primarily designed to maintain law and order and not really for smoothing the path of progress.

The Indian Administrative Service (IAS) organised as the successor service, was patterned on the Indian Civil Service (ICS). It's members today are no more dedicated to the welfare of the common man, than their predecessors were. Late Mr. L.K. Jha, an eminent member of ICS once said that the IAS is clearly constipated and has not broken the mould set by the British Colonial Raj in India.

IAS represented a static view of society, not essentially changing or dynamic said Mr. Nehru. Dr. C.T.

Kurien of the Institute of Development Studies at Chennai, wrote saying Nehru had a wonderful opportunity to build up institutions, which would have demonstrated very clearly, that the bureaucracy he inherited was to be only a limited instrument, and not to become substantially the agency, that determines the priorities of the people of India.

The bureaucrats with their law and order approach to governance, their commitment to the social status quo, and their lack of development experience, and urban management, are hardly an ideal instrument for social and economic transformation. The bureaucracy is rigid, regulation—heavy and remote, is unfit to respond to varying local needs. The left-over traditions of the colonial civil service, place more emphasis on regulating the people, than on creating opportunities for them, to prosper and grow. A democratic city administration cannot be run with the mindset of diehard imperialists.

The system needs to be revamped, not simply because of its grotesque built-in inefficiencies, but because such a system, as experience has shown, tends to miniaturize the common man. Bureaucracy has an infinite capacity of frustrating any reform. It's resistance is resolute and firm. Therefore, what is required is a vastly superior political will and vision to overcome it.

Placement of power in the hands of elected municipal Councilors and unelected officials is inevitable. However, when the power is abused we are justifiably angered, at times frustrated. But what can we do besides get angry? What can we do beyond simply voting in municipal elections and hoping for the best? Actually we ought to be voting, not to grant the Councilors power, but to elect the person who is least likely to abuse the power of the office being sought. Experience has shown that political power has a strong tendency to corrupt. How does corruption begin? A politician's succumbing to the corrupting allure of power is in part, a reflection of ourselves and our society. Yes, power corrupts ! But so do selfishness and complacency. We can moderate the corrupting influence of political power, if we stand for something beyond ourselves and thereby show politicians that we expect them to do likewise.

As residents of Delhi we can be an important influence on the city government. And as voters it is we who elect the Councilors. We could choose not to reelect them if they have not been sensitive to our wishes and needs. As a resident of Delhi, you should perceive yourself as much more than a consumer of municipal services. As a person in a society that has representative city government, you have many responsibilities, as well as many rights. In a selfish way many of us pay close attention to what is important to us personally, what is of benefit to us, and what will help us get more of what we want. While it may be good for people to seek personal fulfillment, as a citizen in a democracy, you also should have concerns about what is best for your city–Metropolitan Delhi.

Life in Delhi, still is very much a proposition of everyone for himself or herself. The moral imperatives that go hand-in-hand with civic responsibility have had little place. Because the average resident of Delhi is simply not interested. The general problems of Delhi have always been beyond his comprehension. To him or her city's problems are the minuscule problems of his or her neighbourhood.

Because of lack of confidence in Delhi's political leadership and the city's bureaucracy, many in the capital believe they can no longer make a difference. Scandals in the Municipal government and vast amount of money contributed to candidates running for city council by interested groups, land traders, builders, merchants, feed people's perception that the MCD is less and less a government of the people. Infact, the special interest groups are deeply engaged in the process of decision-making.

Democracy at City Level

We need a committed leadership in the national capital, an informed public and most of all a shared vision of a future, in which no one living in the metropolis of Delhi is left behind. The harder challenge in this changed and changing era will be building popular support and political will to make Delhi a better place. Majority of the people in Delhi with all too little political power or clout are affected in their daily lives by the appalling living conditions, but are unable to capture the attention of the City Council, the Mayor or the Commissioner of MCD, to have their problems redressed or resolved.

The best possibility for civil rights and civil liberties, and for democracy generally, lies in a restructuring of our institutions so that people directly participate, to the extent possible in the decisions that affect their lives, there is meaningful political dialogue and a range of political choices, the City Councilors are closely connected to their constituents and have an ongoing mandate, authority and power, and the Municipal Corporation is enabled to function rather than left to suffer from grid-locks arising from conflicts among the City Council and the executive branch.

For democracy to survive and flourish we the people must get involved and not remain just spectators. The government must provide the opportunity to develop a better understanding of our democratic process. Perhaps no form of government, said Lord Bryce, "needs great leaders as much as democracy". For democracy is not self-executing. It takes leadership to bring democracy to life. Great democratic leaders are visionaries, they have an instinct for their nation's future, a course to steer, a port to seek. Through their capacity for persuasion, they win the consent of their people and call forth democracy's inner resources. Government must inculcate a deeper awareness of citizens' responsibilities and the realisation that a single individual can make a difference. Where there is little public awareness, the 'do-nothing forces' of parochialism and special interest tend to prevail.

Our parliamentary system has brought forth a unique breed of legislators, largely unqualified to legislate, who have sought election in order to wield or influence executive power. The system, unfortunately, has produced governments more skilled at politics than at policy or performance. They are career politicians. They are not community people, who come in and try to look at governmental oversight. Their job is being a politician without any political philosophy. There is no predictability consistent in their behaviour. They may not necessarily be bad, but they try to respond to everybody, who approaches them, and they spend quite a bit of time working out compromises or consensus, so nobody will dislike them. If their goal is to stay in office, which it is, they have no long-term goals for the city. They have short-term goals to stay in office. If our elected representatives in the legislature were half as imaginative at solving real problems as they are at perpetuating themselves in office, paradise would dawn on the nation's capital.

With better incomes and more education the middle class in Delhi has become important in size and power. This is the class that demands most. The information technology keeps the people in a continuous state of stimulation and appetite for more and better things. This healthy desire for progress maintains hope, but at the same time generates frustration, as the city government is unable to provide the quality of life people expect.

Delhiites have become more and more cynical about the Municipal Corporation of Delhi. They perceive MCD as some unknown entity, out there, out of touch with them and perhaps out of touch with reality. Delhiites must change their attitude. They should not remain insulated from city government. Their elected representatives–the Councilors have an accountability. People must be made aware of their rights and to fight for them.

People in Delhi should be concerned about their city. Become vocal, go to council meetings, write letters to the editor of your newspaper. Garner support by distributing circulars that identify and clarify issues like the need to protect Delhi's architectural and cultural heritage, to remove encroachments from pavements and sidewalks; provide adequate power and water supply; deal with traffic problems, enforce traffic laws; take measures to prevent crime, reduce pollution; provide mass public transit which is the primary mode of majority of the people in the capital. Find out what other cities, elsewhere, are doing to improve the look, the ambience and living conditions. To make things happen, get to know your Municipal Councilor, the Mayor and the Commissioner, who make the key decisions that affect you and the city. Be part of 'citizen group'. If there isn't one, start your own. Start a suburban newspaper either as a group or as a one-person lobbying force, raise the awareness of the community by reporting on all the key issues in depth and by creating a forum in which other concerned Delhiites can speak out.

Very often, people do not want to stand up and put their head above the crowd. Everyone wants something from the city, but no one wants to hurt anyone's feelings by speaking up. People are not rewarded for being courageous anymore. The Press doesn't help. The media at times cover things in a pretty shallow fashion. However, I am sure in Delhi, there are a few people, intelligent people that care about their city. As Magaret Mead put it: "Never doubt that a small group of thoughtful, committed citizens can change the world. Indeed, it's the only thing that ever has".

Remember, we are living in an age of information technology. Information confers political, economic and social power on those who have access to it. In the years ahead more and more people in Delhi will gain such access, as the cost of new information technology continues to decline. As they do, I am certain, that their insistence on greater accountability and responsiveness from the city government, as well as the National Capital Territory Government is bound to grow.

Very often the public is categorised as lay people, by the bureaucrats and the professionals, meaning, who do not know, separating them from the people who do know. George Bernard Shaw quipped: "Every profession is a conspiracy against the laity".

Inter-communication stimulates the process that makes each individual organize ideas and create concepts to become active participants, instead of passive receivers. Friends meeting casually around coffee houses, businessmen having lunch together, comments and criticism at exhibits, presentations or lectures in which people exchange opinions–these are inter-communications. The individualism we see today has to give way to a greater sense of collective co-existence if things have to improve. Citizens' apathy is a major reason why the builder-politician lobby gets away with gross violations. Only concerned Delhiites initiative can prevent politicians from hijacking the agenda and making the already poor quality of urban life much worse.

People generally know bad development, when they see it after it's built. One doesn't need any formal training in planning. One has just to drive around Delhi or its suburbs and look around. There are roads so chocked with traffic. There are those long, depressing blocks of faceless buildings. There are residential neighbourhoods where it's virtually impossible to find a place to park.

Time has come, whereby people who live in these neighbourhoods, who have had enough, should organise, pool their strength, and make their views and opinions heard. People must unite and challenge the developers unwanted, ill-planned building activities, and save their neighbourhoods. You don't have to be rich and famous, to take on the powerful, moneyed development interests.

When people are faced with unwanted, unauthorised development in their neighbourhoods, the first most natural reaction is often a shrug. "I just live here". It's not my job to deal with planning matters. That's for Delhi Development Authority or Municipal Corporation of Delhi or Delhi Urban Art Commission Planners. That's what we have regulations and administration for.

Our elected representatives, generally do not see themselves as advocates for the citizens. They see themselves as an impartial body, pulled on the one side by development interests. Zoning is the way governments regulate the amount and type of building allowable on a plot of land. Zoning regulates: how tall a building can be; how big it can be (density, bulk, mass or square footage). Also FAR (Floor Area Ratio); how much of its ground-space it can take up (per cent of plot occupancy); how far it must be set back from the property line or road, alley or other public right-of-way or easement. (building setback).

Density of building is measured in FAR. To figure FAR, total up the square footage of all floors in the building combined, and divide by the square footage (or area) of the plot you are building on. Example–you have a plot of 4,800 sq. ft. The zoning permits 75 per cent of plot coverage, and an FAR of 3, and a building height of 50 feet. The builder/developer can have a total floor area of 14,400 sq. ft.–(FAR 3 × 4,800). How he gets to his total is up to him. With 75 per cent coverage allowed, he can build 3,600 sq. ft. per floor and go up to 4 floors or 40 feet height. Or he could build 2,880 sq. ft./floor and go upto five floors or 50 feet permissible. Zoning also governs the use to which the plot of land can be put, as per the MP landuse plan.

The Residents Welfare Associations must familiarize themselves (their members) with DDA's zoning regulations, development controls and MCD/NDMC Building bye-laws. In order to recognize violations in their neighbourhood and draw the attention of the DDA.

NCT government should publish booklets/pamphlets on the zoning regulations, Development Controls and Building Bye-laws in Residential land use zones for the benefit of the public, their right to information. You can't fight what you don't know about. Residents Welfare Association get a copy of Delhi Plan and read through it carefully, paying special attention to what it foretells for your neighbourhood.

There must be a vision of magnificent possibilities. History has demonstrated, that great achievements, civic or national, is possible only when all elements of the society are conscious of a common heritage, and enjoy the prospects of individual benefit in a future to which all contribute. Delhiites would find out that serving a cause larger than themselves is as vital to their self-respect as it is useful to their city. The common man in Delhi does not quite think for himself. It is the intellectual elite, that can stir up an urban revolution.

Delhiites must be empowered to become active participants in the city's administrative process. Need to forge a relationship between residential neighbourhood, City Government, Non-Government organisations and the private sector, such as Punjab, Haryana and Delhi Chamber of Commerce, and various merchants' associations. It is a community planning vehicle based on a simple belief, that everyone cares about the preservation and enhancement of their own neighbourhood and is willing to take action on behalf of their home, neighbourhood and the city.

This partnership process, at it develops would raise questions about the way Delhi was going about its daily business. The courage and trust of the Municipal officials and neighbourhood residents to enter into a partnership demonstrates the power of the democratic process. It is you the people of Delhi, who individually and collectively can be instrumental in making this capital a better place to live. The number of people voting is on the decline. But that should change. If you do not take the time to vote, you forfeit your right to complain about politicians and bad government. If we do not play a part in choosing our city leaders, we are leaving our future in the hands of others. An apathetic generation needs the inspiration to help, shape what their city's future will look like.

Delhiites must be empowered to become active participants in the city governance process. Maintenance of democracy requires an educated and well informed citizenry, knowledgeable about the city government and its obligatory functions. Real urban experts are the people of Delhi who live and work there. The way of reinvigorate the city is to unleash the innate entrepreneurial energies of its people. They won't revive until they rejoin the national economy. This means empowerment of the residents of Delhi as consumers, workers, and entrepreneurs, with the help from businesses that can make money as they create wealth.

Our city fathers and the people of Delhi alike need to draw lessons from the 'OATH OF THE ATHENIAN YOUTH', which could very well apply to Delhi's youth.

It would read as follows:

> We the Delhiites will never bring disgrace to our nation's capital, by any act of dishonesty or cowardice, nor even desert our suffering comrades in the ranks;
>
> We will fight for the ideal and sacred things of Delhi, both alone and with many;

We will revere and obey the city's traffic laws and the laws prohibiting encroachment on public property, and do best to invite a like respect and reverence in those above us who are prone to annul or set them at naught;

We will strive increasingly to quicken the Delhi public's sense of civic duty; and

Thus, in all these ways, we the Delhiites will transit this great capital of a great nation, not only less, but greater, better and more beautiful, than it was transmitted to us by our forebears. We must all recognize our duty to change this state of affairs and, more important, our interest in doing so.

There is an awareness and pressing demand for a change in attitude towards the environment in Delhi. Ecology is rapidly becoming a meaningful word to a great number of people in the capital, especially the younger people. The younger generation is developing an entirely new set of values that together with the awareness of the decay in Delhi's urban environment is becoming a movement capable of transforming the human habitat–Delhi. Patriotism that asks more of us than symbolic gestures of allegiance. We are part of a cause greater than our individual self-interest, to which we, too, should proudly offer our services. We should look to our political leaders to welcome and help facilitate our desire for greater civic engagement.

People's Participation

The present ineffectiveness of MCD results from the apathy of Delhiites. Because of their prominence in business or the profession, they ought to play an important role in civic affairs, instead MCD (city government) is left mainly to politicians and bureaucrats, whose value and effectiveness are not always equal to the need of the people.

The heterogeneous character of urban Delhi seems partly responsible for the lack of enlightened public participation or intervention. Human relations in this vast metropolis are largely anonymous and superficial. Here is the paradox of close physical contact and distant social relationship.

This heterogeneity has to be overcome if we want to create a keen and alert community in the capital that can both participate in City Government (MCD)/Government of NCT affairs and apply correctives where necessary. Social organisations as a means of integrating people into an organised community are important. A programme of urban community development was initiated in the early sixties in some Indian cities including Delhi. Its objective was to develop an urban community on the basis of awareness and self-help. Not of taking social services to the underprivileged, but of evoking in them a desire for and confidence in the success of self-reliance. It was both educational and organisational in character. Educational, because it aimed at promoting attitudes and habits conducive to social and economic improvement. Organisational, because it sought to bring people together, to pursue common objectives by requiring, where necessary, the reorientation of existing institutions and the creation of new ones to make self-help fully effective.

This movement depended for its success on the emergence and training of local-neighbourhood leaders, who would help to infuse into City Government a new influence that would be constructive, self-reliant and attuned to the needs and feelings of the community. The common man has too little knowledge regarding the workings and the plans of the Municipal Council. In the midst of a austere and drab existence there is little to arouse his enthusiasm.

Some years ago an exhibition of civic activities was displayed in Mumbai. It was a tremendous success, having been witnessed by over a million people who were proud of what their city had done and looked forward to the promised future.

The initial phase of the urban community development project in Delhi was very encouraging. Unfortunately, the project did not take-off. The ineffectiveness of the city government results from the apathy of the Delhiites. This apathy is evident at municipal election, when Delhiites exercising their franchise rarely exceed 40 to 50 per cent of the electorate. Small pressure groups with vested interest are able to extort concessions that may otherwise be harmful to the community. There seems to be a general attitude of either helplessness or indifference to the defects and defaults in MCD, except when they affect an individual.

This mental attitude needs to be overcome in order to create an alert community in the national capital that can both participate in city government (MCD) affairs and apply correctives where necessary. We must develop an urban community on the basis of awareness and self-help through urban community development programme. The object is to evoke in the Delhiites a desire for and confidence in self-reliance. The programme is both educational and organizational, as it is intended to promote attitudes and habits that are conducive to social and economic improvement. The programme seeks to bring Delhiites together to pursue common objectives by requiring, where necessary, the restructuring of present institutions and the creation of new ones that respond to their urban needs.

The common man knows too little about the obligatory functions of the MCD and the responsibilities of the elected council. In the midst of hard and drab urban living conditions, there is little to arouse his enthusiasm. Set up network of local Citizens' forums in order to infuse into city government a new influence that is constructive and attuned to the needs and feelings of the Delhiites. We need a city government that ensures democratic functioning and delivery of urban utilities and services speedily and efficiently. Despite the deplorable physical conditions, the Delhiites do little themselves to correct the situation. Either they are apathetic or they feel that it is entirely a responsibility of government.

Urban Community Development

To develop community feelings, and shared goals among Delhiites, self-help and citizen participation ought to be fostered. Urban Community Development is not a substitute for government action on a large scale, in improving housing and increasing economic opportunity. It is limited to those areas and those problems, where there is a possibility of self-help. The goal is to promote the growth of healthy, harmonious, and satisfying community life, and to encourage the development of citizens' participation, in programmes of civic improvement.

We need to create community consciousness and to encourage Delhiites to participate actively, in efforts to improve their level of living, develop a sense of civic pride, by stimulating local interest in civic betterment campaign. Democratic decentralization of urban services through the organisation of people's development councils, fostering local leadership. Stimulating and development of a community feeling among people who merely live in a neighbourhood without feeling any ties or pride in their surroundings.

Every citizen can initiate the improvement of the physical environment. Whether it be raising awareness of urban design issues, traffic and transportation or convincing local government of the need for stopping urban sprawl or promoting revitalization of older parts of the city. To bring architecture into some sort of harmony with neighbourliness and with people's deep rooted desire to have a sense of belonging to the place where they live.

8

Creating a Vision for the Future

Despite the fact that the Delhi metropolis is the seat of National, State, and City government, the concerned officials especially at State and local level, legislators, planners, developers and builders do not seem to have or perhaps cannot agree on a clear vision of what the nation's capital should be. As a consequence, the Delhi metropolis is at a substantial disadvantage, in attempting to take charge of its future, especially in the face of massive population pressures.

Effective action at local level, requires going beyond, merely managing urban growth, to developing a vision of what the national capital should become, and working persistently to carry forth that vision into reality. What we need still to learn, is that there is so much more we can do, about creating a successful metropolis and successful lives for its people, than we attempt to do. We continually fall short of the possible, that is out therein front of us, because we envisage so little as possible. We are always under shooting, in what we believe is possible to do. It is perhaps because of our lack of imagination and courage to envision the changes our times call for.

Democratic eras are periods of experiment, innovations and adventure. Our political leaders must rally the professionals, and the people to the cause of experiment in urban renaissance. History teaches us that innovative thinking is always troubling because it challenges the old assumptions and disturbs the status quo. (*Status quo, in Latin, means the mess we are in*). Dreading the introduction of change from the present structure, because of the hostility from those who benefit from the status quo, is a poor mood in which to embrace the new millennium.

No one expressed this creed more eloquently than President Abraham Lincoln. He said: "The dogmas of the quiet past are inadequate to the stormy present. We must think a new and act a new. We must disenthrall ourselves and then we shall save our country". Yes, save India from the urban disaster it is heading to.

It was Francis Bacon who said: "He that will not apply new remedies must expect new evils, for time is the greatest innovator".

The key ingredient in helping to bring about a successful city is forging a vision of what the city can be. We as Delhiites must go beyond specific parcels of land development and projects, to developing an inspiring yet realistic vision, one that incorporates development and change, as well as the protection of natural and cultural resources and character.

Successful cities incorporate many elements– commercial vitality, jobs, good educational institutions, a mix of housing types, adequate mass public transportation system so forth, efficient delivery of urban services–water and electricity, that go beyond environmental and aesthetic concerns.

Nevertheless, how a city looks and feels, how it treats its heritage, says much about whether there is in fact a sense of community, a sense of caring by its residents about its future. Our vision for Delhi, as the national capital should entail both protecting its distinctive assets and creating quality development that builds on and enhances such resources.

The historic monuments, architectural heritage, the Ridge, the Yamuna River, Parks, and open spaces are the natural and cultural assets, what makes Delhi distinctive. Delhi's assets and distinctive character are what inspire people, create a sense of concern and motivate action. We will not get very far in developing a vision for the future, without focusing our efforts on the positive assets Delhi has or can create.

Cities are beautiful, not necessarily because of their buildings or open spaces per se, but more so because of the relationship of the buildings with open spaces. It is in this sort of three-dimensional relationship that the city finds its excellence. Like the Piazza di San Marco in Venice or the Cathedral of Notra Dame in Paris.

Delhi is dominated by mundane buildings of little interest. With the exception of few parts, everywhere one sees the ugliness or unsightliness of the man-made urban environment–a wanton destruction through development. Construction of buildings is guided only by the anarchy of individual enterprise and builders in search of quick profits. Delhi–the national capital has degenerated into a city without a soul; a conglomeration of suburbs, most of them non-descript.

Delhi, once, had a special quality about it, but which has since become just another unrecognizable part of a larger, amorphous, sprawling metropolitan area. Steadily, perceptibly, not only Delhi but our other cities are losing the distinctive qualities they once possessed.

The enormous pressure of massive urban growth and development, and consequential effects on the urban landscape are overwhelming. We urgently need to find effective strategies that will enable the metropolis of Delhi to develop in ways that enhance, not degrade the qualities that lend it distinction and character. What makes a city successful, rests largely in the eye of the beholders. It is more a subjective judgement and a feeling, than quantifiable factors and data. Let us then ask ourselves– is Delhi a good place, to live, to work, to raise a family, to enjoy leisure time? These are commonly the needs fulfilled by cities considered successful.

Historic-cultural Preservation

Delhi has significant historical and cultural resources that, properly protected, can significantly enhance its livability and distinctiveness. Lack of public appreciation of the value of preserving local historic and cultural resources, contribute to the threat of demolition and degradation of these resources. The Plan for Delhi should document the numerous values, to the people of Delhi, of its historic and cultural resources, and articulate priority for preserving these resources.

We should have a cultural policy, which must be concerned with the preservation and transmission of the best of our heritage, works that have been ratified by the test of time.

River Yamuna–Protecting and Enhancing it

Historically, rivers have been the birthplace of world's great civilizations. Delhi was born on the banks of the river Yamuna. The river Yamuna is the birthplace of Delhi and serves as a principal source of water supply for the nation's capital. Given the central importance of the Yamuna to local development, it is a key asset, and provides a good focus around which to build local conservation and growth management efforts. Protecting Yamuna and lands adjacent to it serves multiple public objectives, namely:

Protecting people and property from flood damages; protecting quantity and quality of water for public drinking supply; protecting fish and wildlife habitat; and promoting scenic and recreational values.

Seventy per cent of the effluents drain into Yamuna untreated. Yamuna is polluted by untreated effluents. The threats to River Yamuna are numerous: Pollution/ contamination; Loss of public access due to inappropriate river front development; impervious urban surfaces that increase runoff and flood hazards during rainy season; increased turbidity and sedimentation due to soil erosion. We need a local river protection programme, for water is a basic necessity of life for the Delhiites. Clean water supply is critical to public environmental health. A comprehensive programme to protect and enhance Yamuna River resources. Focus attention on protecting an entire watershed. The Yamuna river-front has no public amenity. The river bank is commonly the site of–leaving the people cut-off from their river.

Urban Strategy

Metropolitan Delhi has grown chaotically into an amorphous mass of urban sprawl, forming a conurbation—a complex of suburbs and smaller domitory townships, extending beyond the boundaries of NCT of Delhi, into the adjoining States of Uttar Pradesh and Haryana, destroying the surrounding landscape and leaving large internal areas of deterioration.

The chaos and waste with which the nation's capital has extended, poses a challenge to our concept of health, happiness and welfare. Such an urban pattern or form has destroyed our very perception of home and family. Delhi's urban form derives from simply the addition of undifferentiated parts, without any philosophical guiding principles.

The post-independence suburban development, by the Central Public Works Department, private developers, cooperative housing societies and the Delhi Development Authority, is the driving force behind the decline of Delhi's traditional urban and small city life. About 5 million people live in about one million DDA flats, DDA facilitated settlements, and group housing colonies. DDA has built dreary public housing–characterless flats, facades musty with mildew have cropped up like weeds all over the metropolis.

These suburban residential areas, irrespective of the income level of the residents, have no identity or a sense of place. The metropolis has grown guided only by the anarchy of individual enterprise and builders in search of quick, wind-fall profits. The domitory suburbs of popular housing estates, or colonies growing around Delhi, offer all the drawbacks, and none of the advantages of either city or countryside. They nullify the reduction of working hours by adding to the time taken to travel between house and workplace, the dismal legacy of motorised civilisation of this century.

In order to obviate the vastness and lack of differentiation in the 'megalopolis' into which the nation's capital finds itself, a clearly definable unit of urban life will have to be deviced, that might serve as a cell of a restructured Delhi. We need counter-movement, directed against metropolitan congestion and the urban sprawl. The relief of congestion is not a matter of widening or expanding the suburban areas, but a decentralising all its functions, decentralising urban development in relatively self-contained urban units, responsive to direct human contact and enjoying both urban and rural advantages or benefits.

The urban structure or form recommended for Delhi in the very first Master Plan, 1962 by Town Planning Organisation of the Central Ministry of Health, was to form all new developments, and reform old ones, on the basis of the urban unit, referred to as 'District', as a relatively self-contained unit for daily purposes and needs of the Delhiites, such as employment, shopping, health, education, recreation and cultural activities. The nucleus of the District was to be the 'District Centre'. Fourteen District Centres were proposed, for the entire urban area of Delhi, each District with a population size of one to one and a half lakh people.

The locational relationship was of overriding importance, in greatly minimising the demands on the cost of transportation and urban highways, both in capital as well as recurring maintenance cost. While quite a few of the 14 District Centres have been built, their contents do not reflect the daily needs of the population of the District.

What should be an ideal design for the future urban structure of Delhi-megalopolis is beyond the scope of this book. There are no simplistic or readymade solutions.

However, the way I see it is that the quest for a better or more livable city, must begin with the smallest and most human-unit of urban life.

Conceptual Urban Structure

The formation of the city was due in the beginning, to man's ability to walk over a certain area, within a reasonable period of time. This led to a city which can be enclosed within a square of 2000 yards.

When increasing numbers of people could no longer be accommodated within the small city of the past, growth led to the metropolis. However, the metropolis could not operate properly until it was organised into a system of small cities or townships.

Delhi continues to expand to astronomical figure–15 million people. This growth has to be accommodated by better planning and organisation than has been known in the past. To expand the suburban sprawl beyond into exurbias would overload the city centre with more central functions and increase the problems of congestion. Instead we need to resort to a form of urban design, which rather than segregating urban uses, integrates all essential community needs and activities, within several "urban districts". Each of these districts is conceived of as a traditional township, self-sufficient in education, health services, shopping, employment and leisure.

Unfortunately, Delhi metropolis does not have a structure serving its increasing complexity, in the same way as the structure of the past served the complexity existing in those days.

It is neither the size nor rate of growth of Delhi metropolis alone is the cause of the urban problem, instead it is the lack of proper structure for the national capital. Delhi metropolis cannot operate properly unless it is organised into a system of small townships. We need to divide the metropolis into physical units of optimum size, which will lay the foundation for the organisation of future Delhi.

Growing experience in municipal administration has pointed out the need, not only for more coordination over a broader area of the national Capital, but also for a greater degree of decentralisation in the decisions and programmes which directly affect the everyday lives of Delhiites.

In order to achieve these objectives, an appropriate self-contained community pattern, served by an adequate transportation system, needs to be developed. The structure should be hierarchical, with the bigger unit the 'District' with the District Centre like Nehru Place for instance as its nucleus; followed by the 'Community' with Community Centre, such as Yashvant Place as its nucleus; and lastly the Residential neighbourhood with the residential shopping complex as its nucleus.

The hierarchical structure provides considerable degree of relative self-containment and because of their population size are able to support a wide variety of local facilities and services. Moreover, the physical dimensions they usually assume fall within the human-scale. With these endowments, they also provide a viable basis on which to build effective local community decision-making and programme-administration in matters of primarily local concern. The community life must be organised in such a way as to minimize the distance between residents and the facilities that serve them.

In Delhi, the transition to such an urban design or urban structure would entail difficulties and high costs, since all the land within miles of the central city is already developed. Nevertheless, much can be done to restructure Delhi Metropolis, through urban renewal to regroup activities into balanced urban districts.

Cities-within-cities concept of urban design, could provide answer to restoring Delhi metropolis to the human scale by breaking down of the vast spread out metropolis into social units. To quote Lewis Mumford "the city must be planned to the human scale. A fully human existence requires an environment built to human scale. But what is a human scale? In order to obviate the vastness and lack of differentiation in the metropolitan city like Delhi we must devise a clearly definable unit of urban life, that might serve as the cell of a restructured urban organisation.

The search for a better or more livable city must, therefore, begin with the smallest and most human unit–the residential neighbourhood–the traditional mohalla or a wada of the old cities in India. Despite technological progress, people are still limited to the human scale in their way of living. We must respect and renew our ancient traditional pattern of community life–the 'neighbourhood' concept, intended to localise the daily life of the residents. In such neighbourhoods, through traffic would be routed outside along the peripheral roads, while the inner streets would serve only as access to the houses.

The neighbourhood unit concept was first developed by Clarence Perry and published in his work on the Regional Survey of New York and its environs in the year 1929. The concept was adopted by a distinguished

American urban planner, Clarence Stein in pioneering urban design the 'Radburn Plan'. Lewis Mumford a notable advocate of the neighbourhood concept and in Europe, Stein Eiler Rasmussen were the other supporters of the concept.

The concept has been applied in the Netherlands, South America and Australia. Planner Abercrombie utilised the concept in his Greater London Plan. When the New Towns of post-war Britain were designed, the neighbourhood system became the framework for most residential areas.

Perry's principles for the creation of neighbourhoods were, that the unit should provide housing for the size of population for which one primary school is required, its actual area depending on the population density.

A system of small parks and recreation areas, planned to meet the needs of the neighbourhood population, should be provided. Sites for the primary school and other neighbourhood level institutions having service areas coinciding with the limits of the neighbourhood area, should be suitably grouped at a central point. Shopping centre is to be placed on the circumference of the neighbourhood. The neighbourhood should be bounded on all sides by arterial roads, and the street-system as a whole should be designed to facilitate traffic movement within the neighbourhood and to discourage its use by through traffic.

Perry stated that these principles will result in a community of people in which the fundamental needs of family life will be met more completely than by the usual type residential areas. Perry's neighbourhood should give its residents a sense of identification and belonging, and this is the beginning of a community feeling.

Apart from being neighbourhood units within which many of the basic family needs are met, the unit is a valuable areal tool and index for the urban planner. Thereby the metro-city of Delhi can be planned as a series of related organisms which are in some ways independent of and in other ways dependent upon each other.

The neighbourhood is also a basic unit for assessing and evaluating various elements in the Master Plan. Such elements which are linked with the people and the areas in which they live, including the population pattern and density; schools; parks and recreation; community and cultural activities; religious places; shopping and commercial outlets; transportation; public mass transit and street system; utilities and services; housing, health and welfare.

The neighbourhood is an invaluable guide for development of new residential areas. By planning in advance, there is much more likelihood that adequate and well-sited schools, parks, shopping and community facilities will be provided, and an economical safe and efficient street-system designed. Redevelopment is equally benefitted by the use of the neighbourhood concept.

Traffic Safety in the Neighbourhood

In designing a traffic movement or circulation system in the neighbourhood the planner must consider: who are the users? What are the means of circulation? Where is the access required? What is the effect of the location of road alignments and pedestrian walkways or footpaths on the desired land use pattern and arrangement or placement of buildings?

Primarily the users are residents of the neighbourhood who will use the street system for all the daily activities, secondly, for deliveries and collection of goods, for protective services like fire, police and ambulance; for maintenance and repair.

The means or the modes of circulation are pedestrians, cars, two-wheelers, trucks, bycycles and public transport.

The access is also required from the outside to the neighbourhood; access to abutting houses; and access to various neighbourhood community facilities.

Directness of access, increased speed of through travel, reduction of accidents hazards and elimination of unnecessary traffic from the neighbourhood should be fostered by a clearly well-defined, articulated street pattern. This should be composed of various types of streets, each designed for the character and volume of its traffic, based on the following classification—

Residential street—to provide direct access to the abutting residences;

Neighbourhood feeder street—to connect residential streets to each other, to community facilities and to minor traffic arteries, serving only the residential traffic.

Major traffic street—to connect major urban centres in Delhi metropolis, serving large volumes of long-distance, fast moving traffic, including urban highways.

To discourage through traffic within the neighbourhood, streets should be so laid out, that no street within the neighbourhood can be used as a short-cut between two points outside it.

Similarly, residences should be served by streets whose layout does not invite traffic other than that bound to adjacent dwellings. This can be accomplished by loop or cul-de-sac streets.

Pedestrian walkways or footpaths from residence should be provided for convenient and safe access to primary schools, shops, play ground and parks.

Instead of having to park cars along street-curbs, off-street parking lots as intervals should form part of the residential area layout plan, so as to keep the streets free for the movement of emergency vehicles such as Fire Engines, ambulance etc. There should be adequate street lighting and tree-planting along the streets. The placement of both light poles and trees is an important and integral part of neighbourhood design.

The neighbourhood concept as a clearly definable unit of urban life and as the cell of a restructured urban organisations does not seem to find a place in the Master Plan for Delhi 2021 prepared by the Delhi Development Authority. As has been the practice, the DDA has continued to lay emphasis on the statutory land use plan, which needless to say is necessary, as a policy on how the land in the metropolis of Delhi is to be used.

The landuse plan is two-dimensional, where as the development on a particular land use, other than open spaces, has a third-dimension. Therefore, it becomes all the more necessary for DDA's planners to formulate urban design guidelines or principles on the basis of which detail planning of residential neighbourhoods can be undertaken by developers.

Cities do not deteriorate overnight, and similarly, are not reborn overnight. Urban Planners need to test the possibility of creating a viable urban form for the nation's capital, by building an experimental model that would set a new pattern for future development. This is essential, because the formless growth of Delhi is neither economical nor satisfactory. To plan for an alternative to the amorphous mass of urban sprawl that metropolitan Delhi has become–we must radically revive our concept of urban planning. The planners must change constant urban expansion of piecemeal addition to orderly decentralisation in self-contained "townships" to halt the continued congestion and expansion of the capital which is spilling over into Haryana and UP. Need to evolve a concept to guide the transformation of our suffocating national capital.

We need to develop a prototype of urban form for Delhi. Planners of today must have imaginative and courageous views our changing times require. We have to accept the inevitability of Delhi Metropolis, of a size, not previously seen in world history. In this context, the problems of the immediate future would cluster around finding an efficient metropolitan design, one that would solve the social and physical problems of 'Delhi megapolis'. Planned megapolises, Richard Meier argues, would be far preferable to the haphazard growth of urban conurbation. Meier's solution to the design problem is the Cellular Megapolis each cell taking the form of an 'urban village'.

Jorge Arango in his book "The Urbanisation of the Earth", suggests a system of self-contained urban units, integrated with open land, making possible and practical the control of city growth in both quantity and quality. When the city needs to grow, it creates new urban units. His urban unit is a sector of approximately two square miles, of homogeneous character. (Two square miles means a 15-minute walk from the farthest point to the centre). The Urban Units are separated from one another by Green Channels, the interurban landscape, open land from 1800 feet to one half mile wide, where the main lines of transportation, communications, and services are inconspicuously laid.

System must be adaptable to existing urban pattern of Delhi so that it can be applied without interference to its normal functioning, and in the amount and at the speed proportionate to Delhi's needs and means. The benefits should be felt from the beginning even when started in a modest and limited way. It is not a plan per se, rather it is a way in which city should be organised so that it can be planned. It is a strategy for giving the city a more developed organisation.

In Delhi of the past, people met easily by walking to the central civic places or to one another's shops and homes. In present Delhi, people cannot meet. Distances are too great, traffic too difficult, and public spaces inadequate to contain the crowds, much less their transportation vehicles. Centralization of commercial facilities belong to the past. The scattered shopping centres of today fill the need better. The need for most of people in Delhi to meet casually for interaction and inter communication does exist. It is essential, therefore, to provide the places, wherein urban culture is generated through meetings, exhibits. If there are no such centres and people do not meet, the city and its people become a mediocre mass.

New Urbanism

James Howard Kunstler in his book 'Home from Nowhere' talks about creating an alternative model of the human habitat for the twenty first century–a model of the everyday environment. The model is structured on the principle of the basic unit of planning, being the residential neighbourhood. A cluster of neighbourhoods becomes a bigger town. Clusters of a great many neighbourhoods become a city. The population of a neighbourhood can vary, depending on local conditions. The neighbourhood is limited in physical size, which is defined as a five-minute walking distance or a quarter-mile radius. Human scale is the standard for proportion in buildings and their accessories. Cars and other vehicles are permitted, but do not take precedence over human needs, including aesthetic needs. The neighbourhood contains a public transit stop.

The secondary units of assembly are corridors and districts. Corridors form the boundaries between neighbourhoods, both connecting and defining them. Corridors can incorporate natural feature like drainage channels, green spaces, parks; travel corridors, and railway lines. In cities, a neighbourhood or parts of neighbourhoods can comprise a district depending on the size of the neighbourhood. The street pattern is conceived as a network in order to create the greatest number of alternative routes from one part of the neighbourhood to another. This has the beneficial effect of relieving traffic congestion. The street exist in a hierarchy from wide boulevards to narrow lanes. Thorough fares are distinguished by their character as well as capacity.

Human Habitat

We ought to know-how to assemble a human habitat of high quality, that equitably allows people of all classes to get around in a dignified, comfortable, even pleasurable manner, that gives our children an elderly equal access to civic institutions, that produces safe neighbourhoods for the residents, that honours what is beautiful, and which doesn't destroy its rural and agricultural surroundings.

There is an urgent need to take a hard look at how we create physical environments. It calls for a more dynamic, more inclusive design process. What would make Delhi a better place than it is at present? How do we know and who gets to decide?

Technology oriented investments of the future, will go to those cities in India, that can attract the nation's college educated workforce, which puts a premium on cities perceived as good places to live and work. While current trends will influence the future, it is the very place of change, technological innovations, and economic transformation that are likely to shape the next several decades of the new millennium in ways that seem hard to imagine. We find ourselves living in an era of extraordinary transition, not just technological, but also psychological. Such times call for the new breed of political leadership, armed with a vision and agenda for taking our country along new paths to meet the challenge, particularly that run-away urbanisation poses and the commitment made to the people of India of building a modern nation.

Urban dispersal in Delhi metropolis is a response to the growth and congestion in the central city. We cannot force a reversal of the desire to disperse, instead we have to create new centres of concentration within dispersed suburbia. The future Delhi metropolis must be a place with multiple centres integrating work, commerce, culture and social services.

To make Delhi a better place to live and work in, it must be the engine of progress and the source of culture, education and wealth, where the inhabitants can find remunerative jobs, and where they can acquire adequate housing. To make Delhi a better place, a partnership must be forged among private and public sectors, non-governmental organisations, professional institutions like Institute of Town Planners, India and Indian Institute of Architects, academic communities, representatives of Parliament from Delhi, State Legislators, Municipal Councillors and all those interested in improving Delhi.

Above all, we need new vision, long-term perspective and bold leadership to succeed.

In our future vision for Delhi metropolis, natural as well as environmental assets have to be sustained in the development process, and in doing so we must ensure that the needs of the Delhiites are met. The important thing is of meeting the needs of the present generation without compromising the ability of future generations to meet their own needs. This is what sustainable development is all about. It places people at the very centre of all concerns. It is about developing human capabilities and of providing opportunities for people to make maximum contributions to their own and social development. It is participatory and community based. It aims to mobilise all sectors of the civil society.

A commitment to sustainable development (a new paradigm in development process) by our local city or metropolitan government would mean including additional functions beyond those that are the traditional concerns of local governments in India.

9

Epilogue

Despite economic prosperity, remarkably, little constructive attention has been paid to environmental aspects of social and economic change in the nation's capital, which has degenerated from being a gracious and leisurely city to an urban blight.

Urban crisis facing Delhi has reached threatening proportions, and is becoming more menacing everyday. The extent of the crisis is not being fully appreciated and recognised by the Government of National Capital Territory of Delhi, nor by the Municipal Corporation of Delhi or the Delhi Development Authority. Rather the urban crisis is seen as the crisis related to a single symptom, which causes the worst problems; be it the system of traffic and transportation; a crisis in frequent power outages; inadequate water supply; or in the quality of air. It is certainly not being viewed as a crisis affecting the whole urban system of Delhi metropolis.

The powers that be must mobilise human knowledge to grasp the urban problems, especially the ones affecting the day-to-day lives of the Delhiites and to analyse and understand the metropolis and its crisis, and then develop the right ideas and methods, about how to resolve them, which are meaningful to all sectors concerned, whether government or private. As Delhiites, we must also take responsibility, not only for solving the problems that exist, but also for planning to realise our dreams for the future.

Ours is an age of information technology, unmatched in human experience. The more fortunate few in the capital, are almost propelled toward a future, enriched by computers, communication, and life sciences. But for the many, the glittering opportunities of the Twenty-First Century are beyond reach. In the mega-city of Delhi, most live impoverished lives, lacking the means or awareness to address problems of life in crowded Delhi metropolis; inadequate food and shelter for many, unsafe water, and disease. We face tremendous challenge, as Delhi's population soars.

The most important challenge is to share opportunities and responsibilities between the haves and have-nots. For a metropolis, where the chasm between rich and poor grows wider, will be neither stable or secure. So far we have not made enough of a commitment toward this objective. We should. However, this is a time not for despair, but for a commitment to make the most of our know-how, to address the problems we face in our daily lives. The problems may seem insurmountable, but they are not, because we have the tools, we have brilliant, dedicated people in the nation's capital to find answers. All we need is a sense of sharing and the will to change. What gives our dreams their daring is that they can be realised.

The citizens of Delhi must assume some responsibility for creating more human and sustainable metropolis. All of us have basic rights, however, we must protect the rights of others. Retreat from considering your own interest, but contribute actively to the common good. This is how solidarity will emerge in society. Our obsession with individuality might become self-defeating selfishness.

Public-interest oriented organisations must be put in place, outside of metropolitan government, to play a continuing role in the local governance. The purpose is to make metropolitan and township governments more accountable and functional. These organisations must articulate Delhi's needs and influence how they are addressed, and apply pressure to see that they are implemented, and watch over the performance of the various agencies that deal with them. While citizens must mobilise for the task of making Delhi a better place, it is the leaders of vision and courage and ability that must lead the way.

A coalition of urban development professionals, experts, urban planners, urban designers, architects, environmentalists, urban economists, landscape designers, traffic engineers, sociologists, developers and builders, elected officials and community activists, must be formed to discuss issues related to planning and development of the national capital and revitalisation of older areas.

The Delhi based National Institute for Urban Affairs, can provide a forum for constructive exchange of ideas and information about urban growth management and promote strategies and practices aimed at achieving sustainable urban development and redevelopment, that preserves environmental quality.

The Institute of Town Planners, India, which was established to advance the art and science of planning, and foster awareness of the importance of urban and regional planning, among general public and elected officials, has not done enough to subserve the purpose for which it was established. The ITPI, must and should address these issues, through exhibitions, conferences, journals and newsletters, directed towards general public and not merely among town planners only.

In Neglecting Cities We Neglect the Nation

Many of the issues faced by Delhi, and other cities in India, cut across the range of central government departments, because cities are microcosms of the nation. Urban oriented programmes are administered, through several departments of the Central Ministries, with little or no effort to coordinate them. With the cabinet-level position for the Urban Development Ministry at the Centre, one might assume, would allow a cohesive approach, and would elevate urban policy making to a degree, that it could receive regular attention. But this is not happening. The Ministry of Urban Development at the Centre has been working in a urban policy vacuum, and it has not been the best advocate for the concerns of cities in India.

Urban development, though a local responsibility, it is a national concern, making some form of large-scale urban planning and reconstruction a national imperative. Delhi, like other sister cities, is primarily victim of national trends and conditions beyond its control. These factors are urbanisation, budgetary allocations, an aging infrastructure, and national economic conditions and policies.

Therefore, it is very much in the national interest for the Central government to assist Delhi. For Delhi, like other great cities of India, is the engine that drives nation's economy and laboratory of social and economic experimentation, where most people work, where most jobs are created, where most of the new businesses are born and where most of the national wealth is created.

Revamp Archaic Local Government

There is a desperate need for institutional revolution in India, to meet the challenge of a truly gigantic task of urban development. The entire top-down, rule driven administrative system needs to be reformed. The urban challenge, we face, demands profound structural revamping of existing archaic administrative system in place today. It must be done, even in the face of powerful bureaucratic interests that have often blocked reforms. There is a plenty of inertia and resistance to change, as we see it. The bureaucracy as well as the politicians are comfortable in maintaining the status quo. They are keen to hold on to the power and patronage the present system gives them. Municipal Corporation of Delhi–a jumbo municipal monolith, must be broken up to create a federated system of urban governance for the national capital, thereby bringing township governance at the community level. Key to any urban breakup would be figuring out which functions would be localised at township level and which would be at metropolitan level.

The idea that power should be distributed rather than gathered in relationship to civic governance is, obviously a necessary ingredient of democracy. However, as a fundamental belief it is at odds with a conception of city government that assumes, one must hold power over others and have control over processes in order to be effective and accomplish one's aims.

Those in positions of power often feel that any distribution of power in the name of the community is a restriction on them. Distribution is perceived as something being taken away, as if it were a violation of their individual rights.

In a democracy, at the township level, Delhiites can get involved and participate in shaping the future of Delhi. In fact they will have confidence in the future if they become involved and be part of the decision making process. We must bridge the gap between people and Metropolitan Government, thereby effecting a high quality urban governance that truly is of people. A Paul Valery put it: "Politics is the art of preventing people from taking part in affairs which properly concern them".

Allowing people to influence decisions that affect their lives and the environment is vital for increasing transparency and providing necessary checks and balances to fight corruption and bureaucratic abuse. Such a measure would help in countering efforts by Delhi's economic elite to unduly influence, or even manipulate the policies for their own narrow advantage. The proposed Metropolitan Government must keep pace with changing conditions in the capital and prove its ability to solve the problems the people face day-to-day. It is not only a matter of satisfying the creature comforts of the people, but also of liberating them for creative and contemplative pursuits.

Refurbishing Capital's Image

The Delhi of today is a large spread out metropolis, which has lost its visual scale and has become unbearable in its monotony—a visual chaos. Delhi does not bear an image of a city rather it is a conglomeration of cities old and the new, suburbs and semi-urbanised areas loosely set together. Palatial edifices and squalid slums are the strange complementary features of the national capital, indeed it is the characteristics of all the mega cities of India.

Much of the man-made environment in Delhi is unimaginative and of poor quality. It is a reflection of a generally poor level of understanding and appreciation in our urban society, of the importance of architecture and urban design in the city building process.

Elected leaders in State and municipal government must make urban design a part of their public agenda. Delhiites on the other hand must recognise the profound effect that their physical surroundings have on daily life. The automobile oriented anticity projects like "fly-overs" and elevated roads have intruded upon, if not destroyed sections of the metropolis, wiping out streets and urbanism in their wake. It is essential, then, that we develop principles and techniques to link effectively, the handling of motorised traffic with the designing or restructuring the Delhi metropolis.

The shape, design and character of Delhi metropolis is strongly influenced by the 'international style' architecture. The materials and techniques used in the buildings are often motivated by expediency and economics. Consequently, traditional culture, expressing a social and economic structure, and visual sensibility of a pervasive and unified tradition, is gradually eroded by modern technology and convenience. Delhi shows evidence of different periods in its architectural styles. It displays mixture of styles, materials and scales. (Walled City, Civil Lines Area, Lutyen's New Delhi) and post-independence architecture in suburban areas.

Our own heritage of regional styles and individual characteristics has disappeared. Because of the desire to abandon the past as an irrelevance, so much of priceless value has been lost or destroyed. It is time we rediscovered the richness of our architectural past, as well as the basic principles, which made our old cities develop as they did. Any semblance of traditional character and style in architecture has disappeared, replacing with hybrid, non-discript architecture.

It was Edmund Burke who wrote: "A healthy civilization exist with three relationships intact: It has a relationship with the present, a relationship with the future and a relationship with the past. When the past feeds and sustains the present and the future you have a civilised society".

Urban Transportation

In Delhi we have been building a transportation system dominated by automobiles when modal-split indicates, how important public transport is. To become a world class metropolis and the capital of a great nation, Delhi needs an integrated and efficient transit system. The economy is hurt if people cannot get where they need to go. We must place a high value on mobility in the metropolis; our economic viability is linked by a transportation system. There is a growing public dissatisfaction with traffic congestion, inadequate parking facilities and eroding pedestrian safety.

The automania which has gripped the national capital is heading towards the suffocation of the Delhi metropolis. Urban design conceived apart from its related transportation systems would in the long run be misconceived.

While the Master Plan for Delhi, 2021 has a land use policy, there is no defined policy on transportation which must also include a parking policy.

There has been a rise in vehicle-trips from 45 lakh in 1981 to 118 lakh in 2001. The number of trips is estimated to increase to about 280 lakh by 2021.

Most of these trips like at present, will be performed by mass public transport system. And yet most of the expenditure is being incurred in providing the infrastructure for cars.

How does one "encourage use of public transportation system" as the MPD-2021 stipulates, when the orientation has been more towards the use of car–the individual mode of transportation.

Every car in Delhi occupies large quantities of space for its movement and for its storage. It needs a parking space at home, and a parking space at place of employment. It needs a space on the road and it needs a parking space once you get somewhere in the metropolis of Delhi. It won't occupy all the three or more spaces at once, but the spaces have to be there or using a car, for the Delhiites, will make no sense at all.

Look at Connaught Place, the vibrant central business district of the national capital, where increasing amount of space is given over to cars for parking.

It is estimated that 3 million odd cars and other vehicles occupy around 14 square kilometers of area, which amounts to 10 per cent of the total area of 140 square kilometers of the Delhi metropolis.

This enthronement of the car has plagued the national capital by ill-planned changes that are anti-city in character.

Our aim to achieve decisive improvements of the existing deplorable traffic conditions in the nation's capital is hampered by the fact that most of the thinkers, the expert, the intellectuals are not actively participating in those measures, which they themselves might have determined as necessary, where as most the doers like the DDA, the Municipal Corporation of Delhi or the Delhi State Government are so occupied in action, that no time is left to get acquainted with theories.

Delhi cannot become a world class city, unless we change the way we do urban development, and in particular our current approach to transportation planning.

We need a transportation policy based on rapid, efficient and reliable mass public transit system. Emphasis must be on the need of the people of Delhi, rather than vehicles, in assuring access to workplaces, services and recreational facilities, and on protecting the environmental and aesthetic quality.

We need to put in place a system Metropolitan Transportation Authority (MTA) in-charge of financial and operating city bus service, MRTS and commuter surface rail service. At present the multiplicity of authorities in the capital compound the transport and traffic management problems. The MTA, as an integral part of traffic management, should develop off-street parking facilities, which would be in the form of multi-storyed parking garages at major destination points–like central business districts, suburban shopping centres and the like.

The Urban Underclass

Most people living in the Delhi metropolis, are poor, and most of them live in informal settlements, and earn their livelihood from the informal sector of the economy. The proliferous growth of shanty towns has far outpaced the capacity of existing system to integrate them. These 'jhuggi' dwellers live outside the system in sub-human conditions and in object poverty.

Urban poverty represents waste, the failure to capture the potential output from existing resources. Improving human capital is a much better way of helping the poor, than outright handouts. Mechanisms must be developed to assist the poor, empowering them and providing opportunities to better themselves.

The illiterates are condemned to live an inferior existence, to be isolated from social process, commercial marketing and democratic government. The uneducated Indian is not in reality a free citizen.

The pace and volume of squatting has increased enormously in Delhi. There were about 22,000 families squatting on public lands some 40 years ago. By the turn of the century there are over half million families living in over a thousand squatter settlements (jhuggis).

As the squatters continue to increase their influence and resistence to ouster grows, and as the Delhi State Government-demonstrates its inability to graple with the issue in a comprehensive way, still more migrate from the villages to take advantage of official helplessness or acquiescence.

About a decade or so ago, the Supreme Court ordered clearance of nearly half million squatter settlements. For six years the government of the National Capital Territory of Delhi has been rehabilitating the jhuggi dwellers from different areas of Delhi.

This ad hoc approach to resettlement has adversely affected squatters economic and social conditions. The resettlement colonies lack basic services like water, health and education. Economic linkages of the resettled squatters have been severed, since being relocated forty kilometres from their original squatter settlements.

About four years ago, it had to be the Delhi High Court to express its displeasure on the lack of basic facilities for school children in Narela rehabilitation colony and mandated the Government of the National Capital Territory of Delhi to provide the essential services and facilities. The state government has allowed squatter development to take place, without any defined policy, but are now trying to deal with the problem after the fact, but again in an ad hoc and inconsistent manner.

Prevention of squatting or of increase in squatting should be a primary aspect of the Government of NCT of Delhi. Much squatting can be prevented by anticipating population movements and providing for them. Wherever squatting is inevitable, accessible land should be laid out in plots, provided with municipal services, and designated as future areas of settlement. The designation of specific areas of land on which families may settle legally weaken the justification for illegal settlements (jhuggi jhompris) and for other invasion of private or public property rights.

A master plan should be drawn up for the metropolis, indicating the land for settlement and resettlement. The land chosen should be near work locations or be simultaneously provided with suitable transportation to reach such locations. Squatters should be resettled in localities where they can find livelihood. unavailability of employment will only compel them to seek their own footholds and make them more resistant to resettlement than ever. The objective of the Government of the NCT of Delhi, in a resettlement scheme should not be to reap the best bargain from the operation, but to aid the squatters in their settlement or resettlement and to assume the social and physical improvement of the neighbourhoods which are earmarked for them.

Rehabilitation of jhuggi jhompri dwellers should not be attempted hastily in a single large operation. The processes can be speeded only after some successful examples of resettlement gives further promise of achievement. Resettlement schemes, such as the ones attempted in Delhi, bring frustration to the settlers, generate suspicion, encourage deeper entrenchments into existing footholds, and spur resistance to displacement. One successful clearance weakens the hold of squatters in other areas.

Formulation and execution of a 'squatter settlement' policy requires a concerted effort at all levels of Delhi Government. The policy will require freedom from political interference with those trying to do the job.

Squatter policies call for firmness with understanding. Squatters will settle where they can if they are not told where they can if they are not told where they may. They will build what they can afford if they are not helped to build where and what they should. There should be less concern about what squatters will build than where they will build it, how the land is planned and whether essential utilities and services are available. Initial layout is more important than initial standards of construction.

Delhi Governments move to conduct a pilot project to provide housing units for slum dwellers by forming cooperatives is commnedable as a first step to resolving the housing problems of the squatters.

Under the project, land will be allotted by the State Government's slum department for rehabilitation of about 450 jhuggis on one hectare. The squatters will be provided with one-room tenament and form cooperatives to reduce the possibility of illegal transfer of tenament.

The squatters if guided and helped can often provide constructive examples of free enterprise at work. Having come to an urban life, these people living in jhuggis wish to improve themselves, both economically and socially. For instance, the jhuggis are built by those who live in them. They are not expressions of despair, but of hope and activity and courage. All the evidence points to a high degree of organisation and consciousness of neighbourliness in the jhuggi-jhompris. They will improve with time and with better economic conditions, particularly if the squatters are given a stake in the society and the incentive of ownership.

Delhi's economy does not develop jobs suitable for a critical portion of our urban population. Consequently, urban poor are compelled to engage in inefficient, low-productivity tasks, because of lack of better opportunity. The distinction must be made between different pools of labour. Those engaged in short-term construction jobs and those engaged in long-term production and service jobs. Whatever we do about rebuilding Delhi, won't matter without more long-term productive jobs for minimally educated and minimally skilled. Recognition of this basic economic reality, underscores the urgency of redirecting urban development strategies and policies. If the people living in shanty towns could achieve a higher standard of living, they would begin to reduce birth rate. People living in jhuggis with low standards multiply with almost the same speed as their rural counterparts.

Unauthorised Settlements and Encroachments

More than 50 per cent of Delhi's population lives in unauthorised colonies. Six lakhs or more families live in 1,100 jhuggi settlements. Shopkeepers all over Delhi, invariably encroach on public lands and sidewalks.

Illegal occupation of land is an infringement of property rights. Illegal subdivision of land is in conflict with urban planning regulations. Construction of buildings without permission and in contravention of building bye-laws is rampant in Delhi. The continued large-scale rebuilding of residential areas to higher density, than prescribed in the Master Plan of Delhi, has put pressure on the existing infrastructure and municipal services.

As Delhi becomes more and more crowded and more dense, real-estate prices increase, stimulating even more density and overcrowding. Solving the urban crisis in Delhi requires changing the way we plan for and do urban development. There is a need for policy measures to respond to the urban challenge.

Urban Planning

The challenge posed by urbanisation and its ramifications, is how to manage the metropolis of Delhi. One of the earliest response to urbanisation was an attempt to regulate and manage urban development through planning. The planning response to urbanisation and urban development process has itself evolved through several paradigms; from the long-range comprehensive planning approaches to the structure planning. In India itself from Town Planning Schemes introduced in the twenties by the British during colonial rule to the preparation of Master Plans in post-independent India.

Urban planning is essential to good municipal governance. Unless urban planning is made an integral part of Delhi metropolitan government, it will never rise above its present status. Urban planning has to be given a place in the structure of metropolitan government, where it will be close to the metropolitan council, the Mayor and the metropolitan manager. Where it can develop a close working relationship with other departments, and being part of metropolitan government, urban planning would be supported by a strong public sentiment.

Urban planning is not only concerned with utilitarian issues such as land use, transportation problems and housing shortages, it is very much about looking ahead to the future, envisioning ways to improve the city and the quality of life of its inhabitants.

New Urban Strategy

Both metropolitan congestion and suburban scattering are obsolete. This underscores that good planning must produce a radically new pattern for urban growth in the capital.

Constant urban expansion of piecemeal addition, must be changed to orderly decentralisation in 'self-contained townships' to halt the continued congestion and expansion of Delhi, which is spilling over to Gurgaon and NOIDA.

The Delhi metropolis has been shaped by, among other factors, the way the planning authority has done development. There is no urban strategy—urban planning in Delhi is limited to controlling the use of land through zoning and development controls. The Master Plan for Delhi by DDA, has no agenda, policy, vision, design or strategy. The present generation of urban planners are timid and often led by their superiors, usually bureaucrats, who pride in calling themselves practical or realistic, where this is too often a disguise for lack of imagination and courage to envision the changes our times call for. We must establish a new pattern of urban development for the capital, by restructuring the formless, sprawling suburbia created during the post-independence era, into neighbourhood communities with relative self-containment. We need to conserve our natural environment and preserve our built heritage. Strategies for the urban future of Delhi should focus on recapturing the look, feel and function of a more human metropolis. Small scale retailing, neighbourhood clubs, enforcement of pedestrian side-walk civility and new urban design may be the keys of the future.

The task ahead concerns the process of implementation, guided by the overall concept of future development of the metropolis. Such an effort can be achieved only through the initiative of all the authorities concerned in the Capital, as well as of all citizens of Delhi, who are interested in making Delhi a better place.

10

Master Plan of Delhi, 2021

The Draft Master Plan of Delhi, 2021 prepared by the DDA, is a third generation Plan for the national Capital. The first being the Master Plan of Delhi 1962, which pioneered the process of long-range comprehensive city planning, not only in Delhi, but also in the country as a whole.

The first Master Plan was prepared to contain a population of 5-26 million people by the year 1981. The actual urban population of Delhi enumerated by the census 1981 was 5.76 million people, a difference of half a million people. The population studies undertaken in the course of preparing the Delhi Master Plan-1962 was indicative of the fact that vast currents of migrants from Delhi's impoverished hinterland could in time bloat the national capital into a metropolis of gigantic proportions. The social implications of such urban agglomeration would be staggering. It was necessary then to devise countervailing policies of restricting the population of Delhi and accommodating further increase in urban growth within the National Capital Region.

From the large city of Delhi to the small towns and villages surrounding, there is a certain continuum. Hence if Delhi is not to be flooded, it will not suffice to replan it per se, but it will be equally necessary to develop self-sufficient number of ring towns within the NCR to hold the job-seeking migrants to Delhi. The creation of ring towns around Delhi would raise the status and improve the position of number of smaller towns in the NCR that are otherwise stagnating. The more the development is tackled regionally, the less would be the surge of Delhi-bound migrants.

A regional approach to urban development with Delhi as a metropolitan core, ring towns and rural villages engaged in a variety of livelihoods, sharing common amenities like transport, electricity, education and health facilities, would bridge the gap between Delhi and regional settlements. While the contrast between them and Delhi cannot disappear, the contrast cannot remain as stark as it is today. The whole purpose of creating National Capital Regional Planning Board was to bring into fruition the development of ring towns and thereby creating a balanced development of NCR.

The NCR Board from its inception has been ineffective while the Delhi metropolis keeps growing. By 1991, Delhi's population almost doubled to 9.42 million people, and by the end of the Delhi Master Plan, 2001, the population of the national capital rose to 14 million people.

With the regional approach to urban development thrown to the winds, Delhi's urban population, with a large proportion of migrants, continues to grow. As per the Master Plan of Delhi, 2021, the national capital will have a population of 23 million people by the year 2021 and its urban area will extend from 685 sq. kms. To around 1000 sq. kms. Delhi already an amorphous urban agglomeration of 15 million people, is heading towards a conurbation of 'magaloplois' proportions by the year 2021.

Water requirements in 2001 to meet the demands of about 14 million people in Delhi was 1096 million gallons per day (MGD). Whereas only 785 MGD was available, a shortfall of 311 MGD. For a population of 23 million people, water requirement would amount to 1840 MGD. So Delhi will have to arrange for an additional requirement of 1055 MGD to meet the demands of 23 million people by the year 2021. This is a collosal task for the city that took decades to create a water supply capacity of 785 MGD by 2001.

Power requirement in 2001 was 3,265 MW, whereas available supply was 2,352 MW. The projected requirements for 23 million people is 8,800 MW, which mean 6,448 MW additional power will have to be generated, which is more than twice the power available in 2001. Here again the task is gigantic considering it took over 50 years since independence to create a capacity of 2,352 MW. Delhi generates only 17 per cent of its demand.

The problem that must be faced in providing for the massive new urbanisation of the future are extraordinary in dimension and unusual in type. The experience gained in building the contemporary western metropolis, far less in population, fails utterly to meet the minimum needs of the urban aggregate in India. Richard L. Mier states that if the urbanisation experience in the west has not established procedures suited to the scale of urbanisation needed in the East, then it must be recognised that the Orient, taken as a whole, cannot assemble adequate tools for urbanisation either.

The Master Plan of Delhi, 2021 has no proposal as to what the design of Delhi's future urban structure or form would be like, to contain nine more million people in the next 15 years. This implies that the national capital will continue in its present state of formless mass of urban agglomeration of 23 million people residing check by jowl in a conurbation of some 1,000 square kilometers—a density of 23,000 persons per square kilometer.

A weakness of urban planning in Delhi was the failure of DDA, which has the custody of the Master Plan of Delhi, 1962, prepared by the Town Planning Organisation of Government of India, to see that it was not all embracing. As changes took place in technology, in standards of urban living and in city planning generally the DDA failed to reexamine the Master Plan 1962 and keep abreast of the times.

The Delhi Master Plan, 2021 is not a Plan at all, but a device for preserving existing land uses, population groupings, and other aspects of the status quo. Land use plan and population densities treat urban spaces as per centages and the people as mere numbers.

In spite of over four decades of planning, unchallenged application of the principle of laissez-faire in the building of urban Delhi has created a number of critical problems like traffic congestion, unsightliness and intolerable living conditions.

Planning must start with and be for the people. What kind of Delhi do the Delhiites look forward to? It is a waste of time and public funds to make a Master Plan unless it is related to day-to-day facts of life of the residents of this great Capital of India, with which the local government has to deal with.

In reviewing the current urban planning activity in Delhi, it is evident that there is relatively very little city planning in terms of starting with raw land. Therefore, of necessity the focus of the Master Plan must be on replanning, of correcting the consequences of past growth and guiding existing and future development of the national capital. It will do well in this process if it succeeds in ameleorative measures.

Adapting Delhi to New Needs

Delhi must be able to cope with the types of problems it is faced with, if not it is unlikely to muster the vitality to handle more difficult ones. On the other hand, it is evident from more than one instance that a demonstration of the will to correct deficiencies in the Delhi's urban environment is likely to spur accomplishment in a broader sense. Though, important as these measures seem, they are remedial and corrective, rather than basic. The fundamental task of adapting the structure of Delhi to the requirements of modern metropolitan transportation, industry, living and even for defence purposes, remains.

The vitality of Delhi metropolis is dependent on the adequacy and efficiency of its roads and traffic system. Therefore, the creation of a system capable of coping with the demands of modern traffic must be recognised as a primary feature of the Master Plan of Delhi, 2021. Because, task ahead is staggering, since traffic problem develops much more rapidly than the techniques for its solution.

For, Delhi in order to remain dynamic national capital, urban renewal must be a continuous process. The problem of maintaining the dynamism of Delhi does not arise because its urban structure may have changed only very slowly, nor because there are at any given point of time some deteriorated or nearly deteriorated parts. Actually, the problem arises because of the many instances where the deteriorated parts have not been removed or replaced, but have instead been allowed to remain as a sort of urban backwash, while the flow of change and development has taken place in other parts of Delhi. The issue is one of assuring a continuity of renewal, and it can be solved only by devising means for preventing the accumulation of deteriorated parts and avoiding stagnation within an otherwise dynamic and vibrant Capital of India.

Delhi's unfriendly urban environment is of our own making, unintensional and unforeseen as many of the results may be. If Delhi is chaotic and disorderly is because we lack the means to achieve order. If most parts of Delhi are ugly is because we either do not care about beauty or are not able to produce it and yet the Master Plan for Delhi, 2021 professes to make Delhi a world class city. If we want the nation's capital to be world class, we must first have reached some general agreement as to what kind of city we want Delhi to be and second we must device ways and means for producing the desired results.

The Master Plan of Delhi, 202 1, envisions "the National Capital as a world class city–humane, livable, modern and eco-friendly with adequate and sustainable infrastructure services; a city based on new technologies where all people are above the poverty line and are engaged in productive work."

Today Delhi is far from being a world-class city. It is neither humane, livable, modern, nor eco-friendly Capital of India. Delhi, functionally as well as aesthetically, is a failure. With the exception of few select areas, most of Delhi conjures up an image of a metropolis in filth and squalor, with garbage littered all over and overflowing open drains. With chronic water shortages, frequent power outages and proliferating traffic jams, Delhi has become an unlivable metropolis for the majority of Delhiites.

Aesthetically Delhi's townscape leaves much to be desired. The national capital has been endowed with rich architectural heritage by the Mughals and the British. Etched and painted on specific areas of Delhi are the tales and stories of man, written in an unusual type of three-dimensional language, that convey to the beholder, more than words could ever possibly convey.

Look at Delhi from any vantage viewpoint. Look at it from the air or observe it from street-level. Walking or driving through it, reveals the viscissitudes–the multifaces of the metropolis. The march of Delhi through time is one that is tinged with beauty, grace and mobility in some places and tainted with ugliness, clumsiness and cheapness in others.

As a World Heritage city, designated to be so, we need policy measures to improve and enhance the aesthetic character of Delhi. The DUAC needs to be re-energised to the vital role for which it was put in place by the Act of Parliament.

If the objective is to make Delhi a world class city as the Master Plan of Delhi, 2021 envisions, it is imperative to spell out the planning policies and principles for attaining the stated objectives.

Vision without action is a pipe-dream. For translating the vision into reality, the Delhi Master Plan, 2021 recommends formation of management action groups, comprising of: Delhi Sub-Region Planning Group; Public Transport and Traffic Management; Infrastructure Development Group; Enforcement Group; Plan Monitoring and Spatial Information System Group; Establishment of

Spatial Data Infrastructure for Delhi; Local Level Participating Planning Group; Common Platform for Building Approval Establishment of the Delhi State Social Housing and Infrastructure Corporation; and Legal Framework Review Group.

The reason for formation of action groups is attributed to administrative and management bottlenecks and conflicting interests in the implementation of planned development in Delhi.

The formation of management action groups' for implementing the Master Plan of Delhi, 2021, undoubtedly a bureaucratic ploy, is a misconceived approach, as it tends to thwart the very process of urban planning. Urban planning does not end with the making of the Plan, rather it sets in motion translation of the plan into programmes–action programmes. A viable Plan is a programme, which must be prepared by the DDA, the authority that prepared the Master Plan. Action programme identify various agencies in Delhi responsible for implementing the various elements of the Plan within their preview for which budgetary provisions are made. The DDA as a planning authority, which has the overview of the Plan, must coordinate the activities of these participating agencies in the urban development programme.

Metropolitan Mass Transport

When fully completed the MRTS Network will carry 109 lakh passenger per day, serving about 50 per cent–60 per cent of Delhi's population. Delhi metropolis cannot exist without mass transportation by MRTS, bus or rail. The high cost of individual transportation by cars plus the practical, economic, and physical impossibility of approximately duplicating the space required by each worker by an equal space for parking his or hers car, make mass transportation essential.

The unwillingness of commuters to use the present overcrowded and often obsolete forms of mass transportation by buses constitutes a major problem for a large city like Delhi. Many bus routes in Delhi are running at a deficit. Probably little real progress will be made in improving the mass transportation by buses until metropolitan transit authority is set up to operate both MRTS and bus service.

Generally speaking, the Master Plan of Delhi, 2021 has not considered the issue of how much passenger travel it should encourage by the provision of flyovers and off-street parking facilities, at prohibitive costs. How much do we gain by encouraging the great increase in car traffic, which the core areas of Delhi are unable to handle.

Will it not prove wiser to direct the spending of funds towards improvement of mass transportation by bus, rather than the encouragement of individual transportation facilities. The Delhi Master Plan, 2021, which has not addressed the problem of traffic and transportation, is devoid of a well thought out transportation policy for the National Capital.

Transportation is the means of making metropolitan city of Delhi function by taking people from where they are to where they want to go. The places where they are and where they want to go, however, are changing. They are not the same as they were 20 years ago. Delhiites now work and shop in different places. Fewer people now make the daily journey to work in the central area of Delhi. An increasing number of people work in outlying establishments and shop in suburban shopping centres.

Therefore, before we spend more crores on urban highways, fly-overs and the like we used to consider the kind of metropolis we are trying to build so that transportation becomes the means to an end rather than an end in itself. An integrated land use and transportation plan is a sine-qua-non to the preparation of Master Plan for Delhi.

The Master Plan of Delhi, 2021 has proposed earmarking of 500 metres wide belt on either side of MRTS corridors for intensive development, which will obviously be for commercial purpose. Such a proposal will lead to ribbon development along the MRTS routes. The alternative to such a proposal is to develop commercial activity only at MRTS Station-points.

In suburban Mumbai, in response to market forces commercial activity got established at every suburban railway station-points to cater to the commuters as well as the local population. The unplanned growth of the commercial activities has created virtual chaos, yet these markets flourish because of the captive consumers they attract.

Under no circumstances should such a commercial development be repeated. In order to avoid it, the DDA must prepare detailed urban design schemes to accommodate commercial activities at the MRTS station points. The approach could be similar, if not, better than the District Centre planning and design approach.

Heritage

Master Plan for Delhi, 2021, recognised the built heritage of Delhi as an irreplaceable and non-renewable cultural resources, giving Delhi its identity and character.

But beyond that the Plan has not enunciated any comprehensive policy on the conservation of built heritage on a sustainable basis.

The two institutions that are suppose to be the custodians of our cultural heritage are the Archaeological Survey of India (ASI) and the Indian National Trust for Art and Cultural Heritage (INTACH).

Of the 1321 historical monuments identified by ASI only 170 monuments have been earmarked for protection. That is the role that ASI plays in conservation. Insofar as INTACH is concerned its role seems nebulous.

The need for the conservation of built heritage is not merely to provide evidence of our historic past, but more so to create a linkage between the past and present and transition to future. Neither the ASI nor the INTACH are appropriately structured to perform such a task.

The built heritage being an integral part of Delhi's townscape, it stands to reason that a policy-plan be formulated for the conservation of built heritage as an important element of the Master Plan of Delhi, 2021. Such a plan could be similar to functional plans being drawn up for Transportation, Public Utilities and Housing.

Conservation of built heritage is not confined to protection of historical monuments, it goes beyond to conservation of areas such as Shahjahanabad, Old Delhi, Lutyen's Bungalow Zone, New Delhi. The concept of area conservation is not of maintaining the status quo, as they are not museum pieces but living cities, rather than retaining their character in the process of urban renewal. This presupposes the preparation of comprehensive urban design plans for renewal as was done for Lutyen's

Bungalow Area by the NDRAC–New Delhi Redevelopment Advisory Committee of which the Author was the member secretary and Chief Town Planner.

Most people in Delhi are so apathetic towards their heritage and so are the politicians and the bureaucracy. The constitutional 42nd Amendment Act, 1976, Article 51A stipulates that "It shall be the duty of every citizen of India to value and preserve the rich heritage of our composite culture".

There is a blatant disregard for Delhi's heritage. A structure dating back to Tughlaq period has been reduced to debris in the Jahanpanah forest near Alaknanda in South Delhi. Kala Gumbad, a tomb located on a mound, deep inside the forest area was earlier visible. Today it has been reduced to ruins. According to National Trust for Art and Cultural Heritage (INTACH), the tomb is in a state of serious disrepair. There is also a well dating back to Tughlaq period situated near the tomb. This well is almost hidden from view. The well is only one of its kind in Delhi because of the spiral staircase that leads to its base. Out of the thousands of monuments and historical remains ASI is responsible for only 170 for their upkeep and maintenance. Since the tomb is within DDA Park, the DDA is responsible for its upkeep and maintenance.

Unauthorised Colonies

Inspite of four decases of planned development, almost half of urban Delhi remains outside the planning framework. The Master Plan of Delhi, 2021 has proposed a strategy to contain unplanned development. More specifically the Plan's proposal is incorporating the unauthorised colonies in the main stream of urban development.

Numerous unauthorised colonies that were built over the years is a 'faith accompli'. However, these colonies not having complied with the planning norms remain substandard. Incorporating unauthorised colonies in the main stream of urban development implies that these colonies will have to be upgraded to meet the planning standards that rest of the residential neighbourhoods in the capital have conformed to.

The 'Bhagidari' movement initiated by the Government of National Capital Territory of Delhi will have to play a key role in the upgradation process, which will ultimately be beneficial to the residents of the unauthorised colonies.

Industrial Policy

The two very important elements of the Master Plan for Delhi, 2021 are land use plan and the corresponding zoning regulations which all land within the Delhi metropolis may be developed with relation to kind of use, height of buildings and their intensity, extent of land coverage, and density of population.

Zoning on the other hand is a legal tool for controlling the use to which the land can be put. One of the fundamental principles of zoning is that it must serve a public purpose related to health safety, convenience, or general welfare of the society.

This underscores that no land use, which is hazardous to health, safety and welfare of the residents, ought to be permitted or permitted to exist in the residential areas. And yet, number of hazardous small-scale industries have been operating in residential areas of Delhi with impunity. There are nearly 900 Chemical units in the walled city.

Unfortunately, the Delhi Master Plan which looks to the future-2021 has not addressed the vexing problem caused by hazardous industries nor is there any well defined policy for relocating them.

Instead of letting the location or relocation of these industries happen without any attempt at direction, it is possible and desirable to use various means of guiding industry to places where it is believed to be in the interest of the area, where there is market large enough to permit the operation of the industry on economic scale. We need to create industrial zones.

What is very significant to the planned relocation of smallscale industries is the industrial estate development programme that was initiated in 1955. The device of industrial estates is used as a mechanism for fostering small-scale industry on dispersed basis. The estates projects provide for factories of various sizes, which could either be rented out or outright purchased. They provide public utilities, including water, sewerage, electricity and telecommunication plus access roads for bringing in raw material and dispatching finished products. Special assistance is given to factory owners, who are permitted to resettle on the estates, including long-term rental of factories and technical assistance.

For 'cleaner Delhi', the Government of the National Capital Territory of Delhi must attack the environmental problems on all fronts and not just making the motor vehicles in the Capital environment friendly. The State government needs to go beyond, to weeding out the hazardous industries and other enterprises that pose a threat to Delhi's urban environment.

Bibliography

1. Miles L., *Colean, Renewing our Cities*, The Twentieth Century Fund, New York, 1953.
2. Collin Buchanan, Traffic in Towns, Buchanan Report, HM Stationary Office, London, 1963.
3. Roy Turner, *India's Urban Future*, Oxford University Press, Bombay, 1962.
4. Spiro Kostof, *The City Shaped*, Little Brown and Company (Canada) Ltd., 1991.
5. World Commission on Environment and Development, Our Common Future, Oxford University Press, Delhi, 1987.
6. Patrick Geddes, *Cities in Evolution*, Oxford University Press, New York, 1950.
7. Hanmer Trudy, *The Growth of Cities*, Issues in American History, 1985.
8. Watson, *New Directions in Urban Planning*, Guptil Publication, 1974.
9. Mitchell, Robert B. and Rapkin, *Urban Traffic—A Function of Landuse*, Columbia University, New York, 1954.
10. American Public Health Association, Planning the Neighbourhood R.R. Donnelley & Sons Company, Chicago, 1948.

11. Victor Gruen, Centres for the Urban Environment Van Nostrand Reinhold Company, New York, 1973.

12. Le Corbusier, *The City of Tomorrow and its Planning*, Dover Publication, Inc., New York, 1987.

13. American Society of Planning Officials, Action for Cities Public Administration Service, Chicago, 1950.

14. Robert A. Walker, *The Planning Function in Urban Government*, University of Chicago Press, 1950.

15. Robert E. Park, *Human Communities*, The Free Press, Glencoe, Illinois, 1952.

16. Institute of Traffic Engineering, Traffic Engineering Functions and Administration, Public Administrative Service, Chicago, 1949.

Index

J

K

L

M